CONWAY
HEROES

COMPOSED BY OLD CONWAYS

EDITED BY BOB EVANS

This book is dedicated to the young 'chums' of
HMS CONWAY and with thanksgiving for their
contribution to mankind. The proceeds from this
book are dedicated to the CONWAY Chapel in the
Scriptorium of Birkenhead Priory.

Previous books by Bob Evans
A Dog Collar in the Docks
Mersey Mariners
The Way to Liverpool
The Training Ships of Liverpool
HMS EAGLET
The INDEFATIGABLE
The Mersey Mission to Seafarers
A Lantern on the Stern
Volume One The Early Years
Volume Two The Later Years
Volume Three The Story Never Ends

First Published 2009 by Countyvise Limited,
14 Appin Road, Birkenhead, Wirral CH41 9HH.

Copyright © 2009 Bob Evans

The right of Bob Evans to be identified as the editor of this work has been
asserted by him in accordance with the Copyright, Design and Patents
Act 1988.

British Library Cataloguing in Publication Data.
A catalogue record for this book is available from the British Library.

ISBN 978 1 906823 16 0

IAN EDWARD FRASER
VC, DSC, RD & BAR, RNR, JP

1920 - 2008

Conway Gulls Window

IV

CONTENTS

*The cover: the artist is Keith Snow, from Auckland,
New Zealand*

Birkenhead Priory

FOREWORD

My association with the men of HMS CONWAY goes back as far as 1961, when I used to visit the ship in Menai to conduct a 'Padre's Hour'. They will not remember me, but I always returned to the Mersey Mission to Seamen in Liverpool with the knowledge that these young lads were truly being trained to 'Quit themselves like Men'. This book completely endorses my impressions.

'Quit Ye Like Men. Be Strong.'

Alfie Windsor (1964-68) has published with expertise a definitive work on the History of 'HMS CONWAY, 1859 – 1974', and it was with some diffidence that I set about the compilation of this book. However, it is obvious to me that there was a need to publish the research of other Old Conways. This is their book.

We are all in truth but pale shadows of probably the most famous and best loved Old Conway of all, John Masefield (1891-94). His love for the 'old wooden mother' was his motivation.

And all I ask is a merry yarn from a laughing fellow rover,
And a quiet sleep and a sweet dream when the long trick's over.

My task has been made very easy by the endeavours of all the contributors. Chapters One and Two are entirely the work of David Fletcher Rogers (1944-45). He worked alongside Christopher J Willis (Old Worcester) as they published the book 'For Valour' on behalf of The Conway Club and the Association of Old Worcesters. I have naturally concentrated on the Old Conways. Obviously Chapter Two has many contributors and they are acknowledged in the script. Chapter Three has just appeared on the Conway web site and is entirely my selection. It could have been at least twice as long. Chapters Four and Five must have taken years to compile and Geoffrey Haskins (1940-43) has thanked those who assisted him in this mammoth task and he has also indicated his numerous sources. I have taken great liberties with Geoffrey's work, omitting the sources of his research into every name recorded and condensing much of his research to simplify the details for the reader.

I am full of admiration for the research and dedication employed by our contributors. Such work is never completed and all of us involved realise that those who come after us can continue to widen and embellish our efforts.

The photographs are also the work of an Old Conway ... they have all the skills! John MacLeod (1965-67) is a professional Industrial Photographer, involved with commercial, architectural and aerial photography. He kindly has allowed his work to grace this book to illustrate the wonders of the scriptorium chapel.

The chapel windows were created by the artist David Hillhouse.

My elder son, Dr. Stephen Evans has, as usual, done a final check on the script ... he is merciless on commas, hyphens and cross references. My younger son, Martin Evans, keeps his hawk-eye on my computer errors and chastises me for impatience. My daughter, Jane Harvey, keeps me fully topped up with coffee and with an ecclesiastical modicum of red wine.

John and Jean Emmerson of Countyvise are ever helpful with their understanding printing expertise. We have shared much over many years. However, there will be errors, mistakes, misjudgements and omissions and with apologies they can only be attributed to me.

As Editor it has been a privilege to experience the contribution that the 'chums' of Conway have made to the well-being of mankind.

Bob Evans

Liverpool

2009

Chapter House and Conway Scriptorium Chapel

The Conway Scriptorium Chapel

PROLOGUE

Sitting in church a few months ago remembering a famous Old Conway, a dear friend, Canon Bob Evans, MBE, said to me, 'You know there must be lots of Old Boys, unsung heroes, who have made major contributions to their country in war and peace, but whose names are unknown to most of us.'

Already well known in the maritime community on Merseyside, as an author and raconteur, Canon Bob has written many books covering all aspects of nautical matters with titles such as 'The Mersey Mission to Seafarers', 'Training ships on the Mersey' and three volumes of seafarers tales 'A Lantern on the Stern', to name but a few. 'Conway Heroes' is about all those Old Conways whose names perhaps are not so familiar to the general public, many of whom may be found recorded in The Conway Chapel, Birkenhead.

But what, some people may be asking, was HMS CONWAY?

In the mid-nineteenth century Britain had an Empire and 'ruled the waves'. The Royal Navy recruited their seamen by press gangs, very often ensnaring merchant seafarers. About this time, the then Board of Trade drew up the Merchant Shipping Acts of 1851 and 1854 to improve the conditions and discipline in the Merchant Navy for masters, mates and seamen. In order to comply with these acts, the Liverpool shipowners set up an organisation called The Mercantile Marine Service Association to train boys to become officers in the Merchant Service.

Following the example of the Royal Navy, who had a Royal Naval Reserve ship based on the Mersey for training purposes, an approach was made to the Admiralty to provide a ship for Merchant Navy training. As a result they were offered the 652-ton coastguard ship HMS CONWAY based at Devonport. The offer was accepted and the Conway arrived in Liverpool on 9th February, 1859, to be fitted out for accommodating 120 boys. This ship was moored off the Rock Ferry slip in the Sloyne and was formally opened on 1st August that year.

Within two years this vessel proved to be too small, so the MMSA approached the Admiralty again and were offered a 60-gun frigate, HMS WINCHESTER, which, after exchanging names with the CONWAY, remained off Rock Ferry for fifteen years until she too was replaced with a 92-gun ship of the line, HMS NILE in 1876. Laid down in 1826 and launched in 1828, she was a second rate ship of the line, 205 feet long and 4375 tons costing £86,197 with a crew of 850. The third CONWAY remained in service for 77 years until she was lost in the Menai Straits in 1953.

Conway was a familiar sight in the Sloyne, and became an integral part of the Mersey scene. Cadets looking out over the Mersey in those days would see liners, tramps and tankers sailing in on every tide, giving substance to their dreams of a career at sea. In these surroundings they learned navigation, seamanship, signals, rule of the road, and all about tides and the weather. Senior Cadets, under the supervision of Officers, were responsible for maintaining law and order on board. Their training instilled in them the discipline necessary to become leaders and take command. Being moored on a busy river, all CONWAY's stores, water, coal, personnel and mail were brought on board by the ship's cutters and motor boats, which were manned and cox'd by Cadets themselves. Bringing a boat alongside in a strong tide with an eagle-eyed Officer watching from the gangway could be a daunting prospect and bring forth some cutting remarks, but that's how we learned our seamanship.

During the bombing of Liverpool in the early war years, it was decided in 1941 that the CONWAY should be moved to moorings off Bangor, North Wales, for safety. Two months before she left the Mersey, the SS TACOMA CITY, anchored nearby, had been sunk by a parachute mine and all her crew of forty-one, including the Master, had been picked up by Conway Cadets.

Shore facilities were limited at Bangor and in 1949 by agreement with the Marquis of Anglesey, CONWAY was moved to new moorings off Plas Newydd, where facilities included a dock, playing fields, accommodation for 'new chums' (Cadets in their first term), class rooms and laboratories.

Four years later CONWAY was lost while being towed through the Swellies, the most dangerous part of the Menai Straits between the Bridges, on her way to Birkenhead for dry-docking.

Cadets were housed first in tents and then huts while a new CONWAY College (a Stone Frigate in naval terms) was built in the grounds at Plas Newydd and formally opened by HRH the Duke of Edinburgh in 1964.

In the late sixties the shipping industry was changing and demand for Officer Cadets was falling. The MMSA relinquished control of CONWAY to the British Shipping Federation and Cheshire County Council, but the number of Cadets under training had fallen to an uneconomic 170 by 1972. CONWAY finally 'paid off' on 11th July, 1974. Over 115 years, it is estimated that between ten and eleven thousand Cadets received training for a career at sea.

This was HMS CONWAY.

Three years before the 'pay off' a chapel had been completed and consecrated in the grounds at Plas Newydd for the Cadets, paid for by contributions from Old Conways and other supporters. All the honours boards, lecterns, and other religious items salvaged from the ship had been placed in the new chapel so when the establishment closed they were locked in the vestry for safe keeping.

The College now became the 'Conway Centre' and was used by Cheshire Education Authority as a short term course centre for students. The chapel itself was de-consecrated and used as a theatre, for disco's and other non-religious activities. Fearful for their safety, the artefacts in the vestry were recovered by a group of Old Conways some twenty years later and a home for them was found in the Scriptorium at Birkenhead Priory, now known as The CONWAY Chapel. This Chapel has now been open for twelve years and is maintained by the Friends of HMS CONWAY in co-operation with Wirral Museums.

The friends of HMS CONWAY are grateful to Bob for collating and editing these memoirs and are pleased to sponsor the book following his wish to donate all proceeds to the maintenance of the CONWAY Chapel. He said "I hope that all Old Conways around the world will help to secure this heritage for future generations," He added that long after we have all 'crossed the bar', the Conway Chapel will be the only tangible reminder of the CONWAY years.

Captain David N B Nutman, FNI (1950-51)

Chairman of the Friends of HMS CONWAY

The Bangor Window

HMS CONWAY

SO PRAISE THE **LORD** FROM THE EARTH

YOU GREAT SEA CREATURES AND ALL OCEAN DEPTHS

JBR

CHAPTER ONE

VICTORIA CROSS, ALBERT MEDAL, GEORGE CROSS, GEORGE MEDAL

 THE CONWAY VICTORIA CROSS HOLDERS FOR VALOUR

EDWARD UNWIN, VC.
CONWAY 1878-80

    Edward Unwin was born on 17th March, 1864, the son of Edward Wilberforce Unwin, JP, and Henrietta Jane (nee Carmac) at Forest Lodge, Hythe, Hampshire.

    He went to a school run by the Reverend Fred Nash at Clavering in Essex before joining CONWAY, which he left, in 1880, after a tempestuous career culminating in receiving two dozen strokes of the birch. He went to sea in a clipper ship, ROSLYN CASTLE, owned by Donald Currie and later with P & O. In October 1895, when the Navy was short of deck watch-keepers and navigating officers, Unwin was one of a hundred Merchant Service officers who were transferred to commissions in the Royal Navy. He served in the punitive expedition to the Benin River in 1897, in the Port Guard ship THUNDERER for the fleet manoeuvres of 1899 and in South Africa in 1900. He retired from the Navy in 1909 with the rank of Commander, but was recalled at mobilisation on the 29th July, 1914.

When the invasion fleet for the Gallipoli landings was gathering at Mudros in February and March of 1915, Unwin was in command of the old torpedo gunboat HUSSAR, which had been converted for use as a yacht and communications centre for the C-in-C Mediterranean. Unwin had been the fleet coaling Officer on Jellicoe's staff in IRON DUKE, the Grand Fleet flagship, and he had special knowledge of the construction and design of colliers and considerable expertise in the handling of lighters alongside.

The idea of filling a converted collier the SS RIVER CLYDE with assault troops and running her ashore was largely Unwin's, as were the special ports and gangways and the use of the hopper and the lighters to make a floating bridge. He was himself appointed to command RIVER CLYDE with the rank of Acting Captain. His plan of using RIVER CLYDE was discounted by more orthodox Officers and it was only put into effect at all through the personal decision of Admiral Wemyss.

In theory, the plan of attack for V Beach, on the southern tip of Cape Helles on the Gallipoli peninsula, seemed sound enough. The battleship ALBION would bombard the village and fort of Seddul Bahir, to plaster the Turkish defences, subdue the garrison, destroy the trenches and blow holes in the barbed wire on the beach. While the Turks's heads were kept down, the RIVER CLYDE would run in, accompanied by a small hopper normally used for dredging mud, three lighters and six cutters each full of troops and towed by picket boats. The hopper would ground on the beach. The lighters would be positioned as a floating pontoon bridge. Some 1000 - 1500 men of the 29th Division, men of the Fusiliers, the Hampshires and the West Riding Field Company and, accompanied by men from the cutters, would disembark through special ports cut in RIVER CLYDE's sides, run down specially-constructed gangways, cross the bridge and storm the beach. There they would advance inland and join forces with troops who had made similarly successful landings at W, X and Y beaches further up the coast, all four pressing on to take the town of Krithia and the heights of Achi Baba to the north-west.

The reality, which began at 6 am on Sunday, 25th April, 1915 was somewhat different.

ALBION duly bombarded for an hour. RIVER CLYDE, the hopper and the lighters ran in and, despite some hitches and premature groundings, the floating bridge was established. But almost as soon as she grounded and when the picket boats were but thirty yards from the beach, the Turks opened fire. For as soon as the bombardment had lifted, three platoons of Turkish soldiers, with four machine guns, returned to their hardly-damaged trenches and their almost-intact wire. So, just as the disembarkation was gathering speed, they opened fire.

In a moment RIVER CLYDE's gangways were strewn and choked with dead and dying. The Dublin Fusiliers in the lighters were cut down where they stood. The catastrophe was past comprehension.

Unable to believe what was happening, fresh men passed out of RIVER CLYDE's hold, tossing the dead bodies into the sea to make way for themselves to go forward to the slaughter. A few men got ashore and sheltered under a bank, but there was no question of anybody joining them. After three hours, 1,500 men had tried to land and only 200 had done so. The guns on RIVER CLYDE's foc'sle could make little impression on the Turkish defences, and the main body of troops could not get ashore until after dark that evening.

That anybody got ashore at all was almost entirely due to the great gallantry and physical stamina of RIVER CLYDE's officers and men. At one point because of the fire (reckoned at one time to be ten thousand rounds a minute), the current setting round the cape and the difficulties of securing the bridge, the lighters began to drift away from the beach. Unwin swam ashore with a line, secured the first lighter and towed it to shore. There was nothing suitable to secure the lighter to, so he stood in the water himself, like a human bollard, with the line wrapped around his waist, while the first parties of Munster Fusiliers rushed over his head. The men who assisted Unwin had to swim from lighter to lighter, under very heavy fire. Midshipman Drewry of RIVER CLYDE was wounded in the head, but still took lines from one lighter to another until he was exhausted. A sailor from RIVER CLYDE, Able Seaman Williams, stood neck-deep in the water for over an hour, under murderous fire, but he still held on to his line until he was killed where he stood. Another seaman, George Samson, worked in the lighters all day, under constant fire, eventually he was very badly wounded by Maxim machine-gun fire. He carried thirteen pieces of bullet shrapnel in his body to the day of his death. Another Midshipman, Wilfred Malleson, took over from Drewry and swam with lines from the hopper to the lighters and succeeded in securing the nearest lighter. When the line broke he made two more attempts to secure it.

Unwin was in his fifties and the cold and immersion were too much for him. Numbed and helpless he was obliged to return to his ship, where the doctor wrapped him up in blankets. But as soon as his circulation had returned he ignored the doctor's advice and went back to the lighters, where he was wounded three times. Later in the morning, he decided that something must be done for the wounded lying in the shallow water by the beach. He commandeered a launch, secured her stern to RIVER CLYDE and punted her to the shore. He rescued seven or eight wounded men, manhandled them into his boat and hauled them back to the RIVER CLYDE. He was in the end forced to stop through sheer physical exhaustion.

Unwin, Drewry, Malleson, Williams and Samson were all gazetted for the VICTORIA CROSS on 16th August, 1915.

After his injuries in RIVER CLYDE, Unwin went home for an operation in Haslar Hospital in Alverstoke, Hampshire, but he was back in Mudros on 1st July, 1915, and commanded the cruiser, ENDYMION. He was beach-master for the Allied landings at Sulva Bay on 7th August and, for the evacuations in December, he was awarded a CMG for his services in March, 1916. He was the last to leave the beaches and, as he was leaving a man fell overboard. Unwin jumped in and rescued him.

He was invested with his Victoria Cross by King George V at Buckingham Palace on 15th January, 1916.

From March to October, 1916, he commanded the light cruiser, AMETHYST on the South-East America Station. In January 1917, he was appointed Principal Naval Transport Officer in Egypt (and received the Order of the Nile). A year later he was Principal Naval Transport

Officer for the Eastern Mediterranean and was promoted to Commodore in 1919. He retired with the rank of Captain in 1920, his seniority back-dated to 11th November, 1918 for his war service.

In 1897, Unwin had married Evelyn Agnes Carew, the daughter of Major-General Dobree Carew of Guernsey. They had two sons and two daughters. In retirement Unwin lived at Ashbourne in Derbyshire and later at Hindhead in Surrey. He died on 19th April, 1950, and is buried at nearby Grayshott.

CHARLES GEORGE BONNER, VC.
CONWAY 1899–1901

Charles George Bonner was born on 29th December, 1884 at Shuttington, Warwickshire, the youngest son of Samuel Bonner, JP, of Aldridge near Walsall, Staffordshire, and Jane, the daughter of Charles Hellaby, of Bramcote Hall. He went to Bishop Vesey's Grammar School, Sutton Coldfield, and Coleshill Grammar School, and then in 1899 to CONWAY. He joined the firm of George Milne & Co. in 1901 and went to sea as an Apprentice in the sailing ship INVERMARK, then as Second Mate and Chief Mate in the barque ASHMORE. He took his Master's certificate at the age of twenty two. Changing from sail to steam, he joined the Johnston Line, serving in their ships in the Black Sea trade. He was in the INCEMORE when she collided with the German liner KAISER WILHELM off the Isle of Wight.

In August, 1917, Bonner was serving as First Officer of the Q ship DUNRAVEN, a converted collier from Cardiff, commanded by the legendary Commander Gordon Campbell, who himself had won a VICTORIA CROSS in an earlier Q ship action.

Submarines had been active in the Bay of Biscay and so, when DUNRAVEN sailed on 4th August, 1917, Campbell made a large detour into the Bay on his way to Queenstown in Southern Ireland. As Admiral Bayly, the C-in-C Western Approaches at Queenstown, said, 'Campbell had a genius for foretelling whereabouts a submarine was likely to be found'. On 8th August some 130 miles south-west of Ushant, he did it again. At 10.58 am, a submarine was sighted on the horizon.

DUNRAVEN played the part of the unobservant merchantman and the submarine did not dive for some minutes. She eventually surfaced dead astern of DUNRAVEN (the most awkward bearing for a Q-ship, showing that the U-boats were growing wary) and opened fire at 11.50 am, at a range of about 5,000 yards.

Campbell made smoke, and sent off frantic panic distress signals (without giving any position) whilst on the poop the gunners on the $2\frac{1}{2}$ pounder token gun gave a brilliant demonstration of poor shooting.

The U-boat (U.71) shelled for about half an hour, without hitting. Campbell hoped to lure him much nearer before opening fire himself. Slowly the submarine closed to within 1,000 yards and Campbell took advantage of a very near miss a few feet off the port side to stop his ship, cover the whole midships section with steam from a donkey boiler, send away the 'Panic party' and turn hard to port, bringing the submarine abeam of him. All might have been well, except that the submarine, now closing rapidly, scored three quick hits on DUNRAVEN's poop.

The first detonated a depth charge and actually blew Bonner out of his hiding place. The others started a fire on the poop so that Bonner and the others had to stay in hiding whilst a major fire raged in the ammunition store immediately below them.

Meanwhile, UC.71 was crossing DUNRAVEN's stern, close to, and was enveloped in the thick black smoke billowing from her poop. Although his after guns' crew might be blown up at any time, Campbell decided to wait until the submarine emerged from the smoke. At 12.58 pm, just as the submarine appeared, there was a tremendous explosion aft. The 4-inch gun and its crew were blown into the air. One man landed in the sea, and the others on mock railway trucks made of wood and canvas which cushioned their fall and saved their lives.

DUNRAVEN's cover had, literally, been blown and U.71 crashdived. Two shots were fired at her, one of which might have hit. Campbell sent away a second 'Panic party' to try and reassure his opponent, but at 1.20 pm, U.71 torpedoed DUNRAVEN just abaft the engine-room. Campbell sent away a third 'Panic party' on a raft and the original party came back and picked up a few more men, leaving only two guns in DUNRAVEN still manned. The fire on the poop-deck was merrily exploding shells and cordite when the submarine surfaced again and shelled DUNRAVEN steadily for about twenty minutes before diving at 2.50 pm. Using the periscope as an aiming point, Campbell fired two torpedoes at U.71 but missed. He then waited, expecting another torpedo, but nothing happened. U.71 had no torpedoes left and could not surface again because help for DUNRAVEN was on the way. U.71 was not seen again. The destroyer CHRISTOPHER took DUNRAVEN in tow for Plymouth, but the weather worsened, her crew had to be taken off and shortly after 3.00 am the next morning she sank, her ensign still flying.

Bonner was appointed to a command of his own, another Q ship the EILEEN, but before putting to sea he learned that he had been awarded the VICTORIA CROSS. On Friday, 6th October, 1917, he was told to report to the Fourth Sea Lord; thinking that he was going up for the investiture he took an overnight bag and his sword.

When he arrived at the Admiralty he was told that the King wanted to meet him and he was to go that night to Sandringham for a week-end with the Royal Family. During the course of the week-end King George V invested him with the VICTORIA CROSS in his study at York Cottage.

The reason for this unusual investiture was that the King, knowing of the danger of Bonner's new command, wanted to present the decoration to him rather than presenting it perhaps to his widow. They had been married but a few months.

Happily, however, he survived the war and became a First Officer with the Furness Withy Line for a couple of months and then, for the next twenty one years, worked for the Leith Salvage and Towage Co., and became an expert in ship salvage. In 1925, as Captain of the tug BULLGER, he successfully refloated the Copenhagen steamer ELIZABETH from a reef at Johnstone's Point, Campbeltown, Argyll. In the Second World War, he salvaged the CALEDONIA in the Firth of Forth and in 1948 he flew to Norway to advise on the salvage of the German battleship TIRPITZ.

He married Alice Mable, daughter of Thomas Partridge of Walsall, at St. Matthew's Church, Walsall, on 17th June, 1917. They had one son, Gordon Dunraven Bonner, who later became a Surgeon Lieutenant in the RNVR. Bonner died at his home in Edinburgh on 8th February, 1951.

PHILIP ERIC BENT
CONWAY 1909–1910

He's gained a VC for conspicuous pluck?
Well, of course, that is often a matter of luck;
And dash of fervour of racing blood,
Will carry him through on excitement's flood.
Held in the bog that grips his thighs,
Wet to the shuddering skin,
Weighted with pack and equipment,
Stunned in the monstrous din;
Visored against the goodly air,
Sucking in acid breath,
He peers, half blind, through the swirling smoke,
For the stabbing flash of death.
So goes he - so fights - and he is in luck,
For someone may note his conspicuous pluck.

Passchendale for Conspicuous Bravery

This extract from an anonymous First World War poem epitomises the mud, the gallantry and the senselessness of the war in Flanders in general and what has so aptly been named as the hammering match of the Third Battle of Ypres in particular. This was the battle in which Philip Eric Bent was to win the VICTORIA CROSS.

Philip Bent was born in Halifax, Nova Scotia, on 3rd January, 1891. Coming to England with his mother some years later, he was educated at the Grammar School in Ashby-de-la-Zouche before joining CONWAY in 1909. During his time in the ship he was highly respected, greatly liked and was to gain something of a reputation as a boxer.

In his last term he was Senior Cadet-Captain Port Main. Leaving CONWAY in December 1910, he joined the sailing ship VIMERIA owned by Hardiel & Co., and after serving his time passed for Second Mate in 1914.

Finding himself in England at the outbreak of the First World War in August 1914, he immediately volunteered for the Army and enlisted as a private in A Company 1st. Battalion, City of Edinburgh, Royal Scots, at Edinburgh Castle. In April 1915, he was commissioned into the newly formed 7th Battalion Leicestershire Regiment at Aldershot, transferring three months later to the 9th Battalion which sailed for France in October 1915.

Writing from France in April, 1916, he described life in the battlefields as follows:

'Life in the trenches this winter has not been very pleasant, owing to the excessive bad weather, which has made our trenches canals, and our dug-outs to fall in. However, the last week has been glorious, sunshine and good north westerly winds: so we are hoping the worst of the weather is over.

Everything is very quiet with us … a few hours' bombardment and an occasional bombing escapade make up our daily routine.'

In the latter part of 1916 he was wounded in the neck, but returned to duties after only ten days at the Base Hospital. As was not unusual in those terrifying times, his promotion was rapid. In December 1916, he was gazetted Major and Second-in-Command of the battalion, and at the time of the Third great Battle of Ypres, he was Second Lieutenant, Temporary Lieutenant-Colonel commanding the battalion, one of the youngest officers ever to reach that rank.

On the morning of 1ˢᵗ October, 1917 the battle of Polygon Wood had been raging fiercely for five days. The battle was part of General Haig's final phase campaign to break out of the infamous Ypres Salient. Polygon Wood, some seven kilometres due east of the town of Ypres and two kilometres south of the village of Zonnebeke, was on that morning the scene of a hurricane bombardment laid on by the enemy on a fifteen hundred yard front from Reutelbeck northwards to Polygon Wood. The bombardment, which had opened at 5.00 am, had smothered the whole area with shells back to a thousand yards. Half an hour later at 5.30 am, the German infantry appeared in strength. The 9ᵗʰ Leicestershire, who at that time were covering the 110th brigade, were forced to give ground.

The situation was now critical owing to the confusion caused by the attack and the intense artillery fire. Philip Bent personally collected a platoon that was in reserve, and together with other companies and various regimental details, he organised and led them forward to the counter-attack, after issuing orders to other Officers as to the further defence of the line. The counter-attack was successful, the enemy were checked and the positions, which were to prove essentially important for subsequent operations, were regained.

The coolness and magnificent example shown to all ranks were exemplified by Philip Bent personally leading the charge with the cry of 'Come on, the Tigers'. He was killed at the objective after giving his orders for reconsolidation. He has no known grave and was but twenty six years old.

At the subsequent investiture held at Buckingham Palace on 2ⁿᵈ March, 1918, his mother Mrs. Sophy Bent received not only the VICTORIA CROSS for his gallantry that day, but the Distinguished Service Order won earlier in the campaign.

In 1923 his mother presented his medals to his old school at Ashby-de-la-Zouche who in 1970 passed them over for safe keeping to the Regimental Museum at Leicester. At the Army Museum at Halifax, Nova Scotia, can be seen a photograph of Bent, a fine handsome cheerful young man and also within the Museum is a small box with a glass top and a backcloth made from part of his khaki uniform: mounted on it is the bronze plaque (known as the widow's plaque) which was given to the family of those who were killed in action. Below the plaque are his Cadet Captain's stripes and his silver Conway boxing medal.

A few miles east of Ypres is the largest Commonwealth Cemetery in the world, the Tyne Cot British Military Cemetery. It harbours the remains of 11,908 service men. At the far end of the cemetery is the Memorial to the Missing; 34,888 names of soldiers with no known graves, names carved on panel after panel. High on one such is the name P E Bent.

In his mother's village of Hindhead in Surrey, his name is to be found on the War memorial in the grounds of St. Alban's Church.

Today the trees have grown again in Polygon Wood and on the quiet Flanders country road between the villages of Hooge and Becelave. It is difficult to imagine the scenes of violence enacted here, but the well-kept cemeteries in and around the wood and where the pre-war racecourse used to be will ensure that Philip Bent and his comrades are never forgotten.

IAN EDWARD FRASER, VC
CONWAY 1936–38

Ian Fraser was born in Baling, Middlesex on 18th December, 1920, the son of Sydney Fraser, Marine Engineer, and Florence Irene (nee McKenzie), but within six months he was in Kuala Lumpur where his father was employed as an engineer. He went to school in Wallasey, Wirral, Cheshire, and to High Wycombe Royal Grammar School in Buckinghamshire and then to CONWAY. In 1938, being unsuccessful in his first wish of entering the Royal Navy, he joined the Blue Star Line as a Cadet first in TUSCAN STAR and later in SYDNEY STAR. In June 1939, he joined the battleship ROYAL OAK as a Midshipman, RNR, for what he thought was to be four months training and was on board her for the July 1939 Review of the Fleet in Weymouth Bay, Dorset. After war broke out, he served in the destroyer KEITH and then went on to as eventful a war as many men had, setting aside his VC. He was in the destroyer MONTROSE at Dunkirk, and in another destroyer, MALCOLM, when she and other escorts sank U.651 in the Atlantic on 29th June, 1941. Then, 'for no valid reason which I can now recall', he volunteered for submarines.

He served in P.35 and H.43 then, on 1st April, 1943 joined SAHIB in the 10th S/M Squadron in the Mediterranean, winning the DSC. In a depot ship party after a patrol, somebody threw a heavy brass ashtray which landed on Fraser's foot and broke a bone. He was unable to go on SAHIB's next patrol, in which she was lost and all but one of her crew became prisoners-of-war. Fraser, the survivor, was appointed First Lieutenant of the old submarine H.44, refitting at Sheerness.

H.44 went to Londonderry, 'ping running' (sometimes known as being a clockwork mouse) for escorts working up. It was a boring life and, more from boredom than anything else, Fraser volunteered for X-craft in March 1944. He trained in X.20 in Loch Cairnbawn before, on 27th November, 1944, XE.3 was launched by Mrs. Fraser. XE.3 was unofficially named SIGYN, after the ever-loving wife of Loki in Norse mythology, and had the unofficial motto 'Softly, softly, catchee monkey'.

The war in Europe being over, the midget submarines and their supply ship BONAVENTURE moved to the Far East. Amongst the operations planned was one that carried the code name 'Struggle'.

Operation Struggle was to sink the 10,000 ton Japanese cruisers TAKOA and MIYOKO in the Johore Straits. Both had been previously damaged in action, but it was believed that they might still be repaired, and in any case, could be used as floating gun-batteries to defend the Straits.

Operation Struggle was to be carried out by XE.1 (Lieutenant J E Smart, RNVR) and XE.3 towed by the submarines STYGIAN and SPARK respectively, which sailed from Labuan on 26th July, 1945. Passage crews, as their name suggested, manned the X-craft for the towed passage and were relieved by the operational crews who were to carry out the attack.

Fraser's operational crew were Sub-Lieutenant W J L ('Kiwi') Smith RNZNVR, ERA C Reid and Leading Seaman J J Magennis. They transferred from STYGIAN to XE.3 by rubber dinghy at 6.00 am on 30th July. XE.3 slipped her tow at 11 o'clock that night, about two and a half miles from the Horsburgh Light, at the eastern end of the Singapore Channel. Fraser and his crew now faced an intricate and dangerous passage of some forty miles, past shoals and wrecks, across minefields and listening posts, through a buoyed boom and surface patrols. First they sailed along the Singapore Channel and then north and west through the Johore Straits, which lay between Singapore island and the Johore mainland. If they fell into Japanese hands, they were likely to be executed as spies.

Navigated by Fraser, who knew his courses and distances by heart, XE.3 made a steady five knots on the surface and passed the Johore listening posts just after 2.00 am on the 31st July. At 4.30 am, Fraser had to dive hurriedly to avoid a tanker and its escort which came looming up out of the dark. XE.3 hit the bottom at thirty-six feet, damaging the logs which measured speed and distance and on which Fraser relied for his dead-reckoning navigation. In the heat and confinement of the X-craft, conditions were extremely unpleasant. Fraser and his crew kept themselves going by sipping orange juice from the refrigerator and at 6.00 am they took Benzedrine stimulant tablets. XE.3 was then just off the eastern point of Singapore island, near Changi gaol, whose grim grey towers and roofs, with the Rising Sun flag flying above, Fraser actually saw to port through his periscope.

At 9.30 am, Fraser sighted the line of buoys which marked the boom and, waiting outside, managed to follow a small unwary trawler through at 10.30 am. As XE.3 worked her way steadily up the Straits at forty feet, Magennis began to dress in his rubber frogman's suit, assisted by Fraser. The temperature was 85°F inside the submarine and the air heavy and sticky. At 12.50 pm, Fraser saw the shore of Singapore island to his left, some buildings ahead, and then quite suddenly the target TAKOA. As Fraser said, "Although she seemed to appear with the suddenness of an apparition, I had the feeling that I had been staring at her for a long time. She was heavily camouflaged and she lay in the exact position I had plotted on my chart".

It was 1.52 pm, when Fraser began his attack. He and his crew had been nineteen hours without proper sleep and nine hours submerged in their midget submarine. But now was the time for their supreme effort.

TAKOA was anchored with her stern only 50 to 100 yards from the Singapore side of the Straits. The depth of water around her was only 11 to 17 feet, but she lay across a depression in the sea bed some 500 feet wide. Fraser had somehow to get XE.3 across the shallows and into the hole below TAKOA. He had already announced to the depot-ship staff that he thought this was impossible.

The first attack was too fine on TAKOA's bow. Fraser retired and at 3.03 pm he tried again. This time he slid XE.3 neatly under the target. Magennis went out through the 'wet and dry compartment' (which could be flooded and pumped to let a diver in or out of the submarine) and began to fix limpet mines to TAKOA's bottom. The plates were covered in weeds and marine growth and Magennis had to chip and clear away for over half an hour before he could place his six mines properly. Their magnets were unaccountably weak and the mines kept floating up and away, with Magennis swimming after them and bringing them back.

When Magennis came back, Fraser's next task was to release the two side charges, each of two tons of amatol. The port charge dropped away cleanly, but the starboard side stuck. So too did XE.3, underneath TAKOA. Fraser and his crew had a frantic few minutes manoeuvring before the submarine came free. The starboard charge was still there. Fraser volunteered to go out and release it but Magennis insisted that he was the diver and he would go. Armed with a spanner, he climbed out again and in five minutes ... the longest five minutes of Fraser's life ... he released the charge. He came back for the second time and then it was full speed for home.

XE.3 rendezvoused with STYGIAN and was taken in tow again, reaching Labuan on 4th August. Smart and XE.1 arrived the next day. Their target MIYOKO was further up the Straits than TAKOA and they had been delayed by patrol craft. They approached TAKOA shortly before Fraser's charges were timed to detonate, so Smart added his burden to Fraser's under TAKOA and retired. The combined charges duly detonated and blew a great hole in TAKOA's bottom.

Fraser and Magennis were recommended for and awarded the VICTORIA CROSS, which was gazetted on 13th November, 1945 and presented by King George VI at Buckingham Palace on 11th December, 1945.

In 1943, Ian Fraser married Estelle Hughes, a Wren whom he had known since his CONWAY days. They had six children, two of whom were to follow their father to CONWAY.

With the war over, Fraser, with other ex-frogmen and service colleagues formed his own company, Universal Divers Limited, to exploit their skills. Fraser was Managing Director and later Chairman of the Company which later expanded into the field of exploration and maintenance of North Sea oil and gas rigs.

The Parish Church of St. James, New Brighton was completely full as we bade farewell to Ian Edward Fraser, VC, DSC, RD and Bar, JP, on the 11th September 2008. We had all lost a good friend and companion.

THE CONWAY

GEORGE CROSS and ALBERT MEDAL

The GEORGE CROSS (GC) was instigated in 1940 during WW II when there was a need to acknowledge acts of outstanding bravery and courage by civilians. It was intended that the George Cross should stand supreme as the 'CIVILIAN VICTORIA CROSS' and so not be undermined by the award of larger numbers.

The decoration consists of a plain silver cross, with the Royal cipher 'GVI' in the angle of each limb. In the centre is a circular medallion showing Saint George and the Dragon, and surrounded by the inscription, 'For Gallantry'. The reverse is plain and bears the name of the recipient and the date of the award. The George Cross, which is worn before all other decorations except the Victoria Cross, is suspended from a dark blue ribbon threaded through a bar adorned with laurel leaves.

The ALBERT MEDAL (AM) was introduced in 1886 and named after the Prince Consort. It was awarded for 'daring and heroic' actions performed by mariners and others in danger of perishing, by reason of wrecks and other perils of the sea. It was amalgamated with the George Cross in 1949.

The Albert Medal was an oval medal, 57 millimetres long and 30 millimetres wide. The early issues were gold and bronze, the later issues were either gold (1st class) or bronze (2nd class). The AM's (gold 1st class) ribbon was originally blue with two white stripes, but was changed to a wider blue ribbon with four white stripes, The AM, 2nd class, inherited the original ribbon size with two white stripes. In 1904 the 2nd class AM changed the ribbon size to that of the 1st class AM, while retaining the 2nd class two white stripes.

The AM's obverse consist of a letter 'V' (for Victoria) entwined with a letter 'A' for Albert. AMs issued for gallantry at sea also have an anchor. The obverse has the words 'For Gallantry in Saving Life' with 'At Sea' or 'on Land' added as appropriate. In 1917 the title was altered producing the Albert Medal in gold (formerly the AM 1st Class) and the Albert Medal (formerly the 2nd class bronze medal).

Lieutenant-Commander F H Brooke Smith, GC, RD, RNR. (1934-36)

One of the Brooke Smith dynasty (1893-1971) … five members over three generations trained in CONWAY. Francis was awarded the GEORGE CROSS in the Second World War. He volunteered for mine disposal duties. Having previously defused six mines, he went aboard the fire float FIREFLY on the Manchester Ship Canal to defuse a parachute mine. He had never dealt with a similar mine before, but with considerable difficulty he managed to defuse it. His medals are on display in the Imperial War Museum in London.

Lieutenant-Commander William Fletcher, AM, DFC, RN. (1919-20)

Lieutenant-Commander Fletcher was awarded the ALBERT MEDAL for attempting to rescue the crashed

Amy Johnson and another person from the freezing Thames estuary in 1941. Fletcher, who was convinced there was still a chance of saving the second body, ripped off his boots and duffel coat before plunging into the icy sea. From his ship, the HAZLEMERE, the body appeared motionless; and at least two crew members thought the figure might be a German as they believed they could make out a tell-tale helmet. The crew watched as Fletcher appeared to support himself on the body before striking out for the lifeboat battling through the waves to reach him. One of the crew said he appeared 'just about done' as the waves tossed him in and out of view. Eventually he was pulled aboard and given artificial respiration, but he never regained consciousness and died five days later from exposure and shock at the Royal Naval Hospital, Gillingham. His grave is in Woodlands.

Lieutenant E R McKinstry, GC, RNR.

Details of his award are not known other than it was for a rescue at sea. According to The Cadet Magazine he rescued people on three separate occasions, including one when Third Officer in the White Star's TEUTONIC. He jumped overboard and saved the life of a naval instructor at the 1887 Naval Review at Spithead for which he received a reward of thirty pounds. The instructor had been knocked into the water by the boom of a training brig.

Sub-Lieutenant Charles Wood Robinson, AM, RNR. (circa 1885)

'Her Majesty the Queen has been graciously pleased to confer the Decoration of the ALBERT MEDAL of the Second Class on Sub-Lieutenant Charles Wood Robinson, RNR, Third Officer of the RMS TEUTONIC of Liverpool.'

While the Teutonic was steaming at the rate of about 21 knots an hour in St. George's Channel on the 17th April, 1893, at 6.30 am, when few people were about the deck, Mr. Robinson noticed a passenger climbing on to the rail of the ship with the evident intention of jumping overboard. He made an ineffectual attempt to prevent him and then without divesting himself of any of his clothing immediately dived after the man from a height of 35 feet above the water, and only about 30 feet forward of the propellers of the vessel. Mr Robinson reached the man and did his utmost to rescue him, but his efforts were met with violent resistance, and in the end the man succeeded in drowning himself. Mr Robinson ran great risk of being drawn under the propellers, and when picked up was in a very exhausted condition.

Lieutenant-Commander Arthur R S Warden, AM, RN. (1882-90?)

Lieutenant-Commander Warden was awarded the ALBERT MEDAL on 25th October, 1915. The SS MAINE loaded with ammunition and high explosive caught fire and was abandoned by her crew. Lieutenant-Commander Warden proceeded on board and found high explosive cases on fire in the aft hold. He was passed a fire hose and wandered throughout the burning explosives, gradually extinguishing the flames. His award acknowledged that his action prevented an explosion that could have had disastrous results.

THE GEORGE MEDAL

The GEORGE MEDAL was instituted, together with the George Cross, on the 24th September 1940. As the George Cross should stand supreme as the 'civilian Victoria Cross', the George Medal, (GM), was introduced as a 'junior' to the George Cross.

The George Medal is a circular silver medal. The obverse depicts the effigy of the sovereign and the reverse shows Saint George slaying the dragon on the coast of England. The ribbon is red with five narrow stripes, the blue stripe colour being 'borrowed' from the George Cross ribbon.

Lionel (Ken) 'Buster' Crabb, GM, OBE, RNVR. (1922-24)

A Royal Navy frogman, he disappeared in mysterious circumstances whilst diving in Portsmouth harbour near the USSR warship ORDZHONKIDZ. The book 'Commander Crabb is alive' by J Bernard Hutton proposed that he was captured and was taken to Russia where he became Captain Lev Lvovich Korablov in the Soviet Navy. The truth may be less controversial!

BIBLIOGRAPHY

The Victoria Cross at Sea … John Winton (Michael Joseph).

Register of the Victoria Cross, This England Books, VC and DSO Volume 1 … Sir O'Moore Creagh & E N Humphries (Standard Art Book Co., 1924).

Dardanelles Dilemma … E. Keble Chatterton (Rich and Cowan, 1935).

Gallipoli … John Masefield (Heinemann, 1916).

My Mystery Ships … Vice-Admiral Gordon Campbell (Hodder & Stoughton, 1928).

History of the Great War Military Operations, France and Belgium 1917 Vol. 2 … Brigadier-General Sir James E Edmonds (HMSO, 1948).

The Battle Book of Ypres … Beatrice Brice (John Murray 1927).

Twenty Years After - The Battlefields of 1914-1918 then and now … Major-General Sir Ernest Swinton (George Newnes).

Gallant Gentlemen … E Keble Chatterton (Hurst & Blackett, 1931).

Frogman VC … Ian Fraser (Angus & Roberts 1957).

The Conway … John Masefield (Heinemann 1953).

The Records of HMS CONWAY … Conway Club.

CHAPTER TWO

CONWAYS AND THE FALKLANDS
1914 TO 1982 AND IN BETWEEN

BY

SOME WHO WERE THERE

This chapter was produced and compiled by David Fletcher Rogers
(1944-45)

The campaign in the Falkland Islands in 1982 showed how quickly an opportunity for acts of gallantry can arise and it is with honour we remember the service given in that campaign by members of our Association. Now that the ship is paid off this campaign was, in all probability, the last occasion that Conways will see fighting service and it is to be fervently hoped that many years will elapse before another Victoria Cross will be awarded. It gives real pleasure that acts of gallantry by former Cadets are recognised by the highest award in the land.

INTRODUCTION

This Introduction is written for those who may pick up the book and wonder in years to come what the Falklands War of 1982 was all about.

In April 1982, Argentina in an act of naked aggression seized the Falklands Islands. Public opinion was outraged not only because it was a fascist dictator who ordered the invasion, but in large measure because a South American republic with its military junta in comic opera uniforms had the temerity even to contemplate such an action, let alone carry it out.

The Government of the Day ordered the liberation of the Falklands, and this was carried out by a superb feat of supply and force of arms in two and a half months. The lines of supply were over 8000 miles, the enemy air force proved surprisingly efficient, but in the end our forces routed the enemy.

Much has been written about our fighting services, but little about the Merchant Navy in this campaign.

This work is primarily concerned with the work of the Merchant Navy, because CONWAY Cadets were trained for that service, though it will be noted that two of its sons were in most senior appointments in the Royal Navy during the conflict.

Which leads us to what is CONWAY?

HMS CONWAY was a training ship for Officers for the Merchant Navy. The institution was founded in 1859 and closed in 1974, when the Minister of Education of the day, Mrs. Margaret Thatcher, did not dissent from the proposal that it be closed. Thus was disposed of at the stroke of a pen an establishment that turned out the type of Officer that was eagerly sought in 1982. In fact CONWAY training proved suitable for all walks of life and some of the highest positions in all the Armed Services, the Church, the Law, Industry, and as Men of Art and Literature, have been held by Conways, let alone as Masters of Ships.

The Association of those who served in CONWAY, the Conway Club, wish that there shall be a record of the achievements of Conways. This small work sets out some of these achievements including those in an earlier Battle of the Falklands Islands. Most of what is written is by participants at the events, though I have 'filled in' so as to preserve continuity of the story.

Though the contributions are by serving Officers who happen to have been Conways, in many ways their story is typical of the role of the Merchant Navy in the 1982 campaign.

There is one contribution from the father of a Conway, Mr. Sydney Miller, a Falklands Island resident. His valued account of the enemy occupation is justification (if such be necessary) for the necessity for the Islands to be liberated.

For those who read this account with the memory of the Campaign still fresh it will perhaps be a surprise to learn of the leading role the Merchant Navy took in the campaign, and it is quite remarkable that they fitted into naval routine so quickly. The expressions 'rasing', 'vertrepping', and 'crossdecking' are now household words for Merchant seamen who were there.

To all those who contributed to this work the Conway Club expresses its thanks.

To date we know that the following Old Conways, in addition to those mentioned in the script served in the Falklands Campaign:

Captain A W Kinghorn, (1949-51) … AVELONA STAR.

Lieutenant-Commander M Manning, RN, (1962-64) … HMS ARROW.

P Hughes (1968-70) … St Helena.

Rear-Admiral J P Edwards, MVO, (1941-44) … Deputy Chief of Fleet Support

Captain J A M Taylor, (1947-49) … BRITISH DART.

Captain H R Lawton, (1951-52) … LYCAON.

The Early Years

Conways have often been to the remote Falkland Islands 8000 miles from England in peace and war. Up to 1914 many Conways arrived in Port Stanley after their tall ships had sustained severe damage in trying to round Cape Horn. Some ships would spend over six weeks in trying to beat up to the West of Cape Horn. They would be in seas so mountainous that even the large heavy barques of 1900 sometimes were lost or severely damaged.

Damaged ships with top hamper ruined would stagger back to Port Stanley, repair uneconomic, there to be left. It is the reason why GREAT BRITAIN was there. The Falkland Islands of all places in the world holds today so many old ships around its creeks and inlets. Some of these ships did not reach the vicinity of Cape Horn, but were dismasted near the Islands, for the seas in this part of the world are probably, and consistently, the heaviest, the highest and the most dangerous.

That is how many Conways came to Port Stanley to depart as DBS … Distressed British Seamen … a term used by Government officials when a seaman would arrive in port with no ship and no money and had to be shipped home at Government expense.

At all times in this story one must remember the appalling weather, the cold, the wet, the prolonged loss of sleep for day after day and night after night.

The Great War

1982 was not the first time Conways had been to the Falklands in war.

On 4th August, 1914, what used to be called the Great War broke out. The German Navy had at that time a powerful squadron in the Chinese port of Tsingtau, but its Commander, Rear-Admiral Graf von Spee, knew his position was hopeless if he remained on the China Coast, so he sailed out into the wastes of the Pacific, destination unknown.

Admiral von Spee's force consisted of two modern armoured cruisers, the SCHARNHORST and GNEISENAU and three light cruisers, DRESDEN, NURNBERG and LEIBZIG. As Von Spee knew that our forces on the China and East Indies Station were sufficient to deal with him, the Admiralty reckoned that he would attack our shipping off the west coast of South America for our naval presence there was slight.

Extraordinarily, only a 13-knot battleship of 1897, CANOPUS, was sent to supplement the comparatively weak forces of Rear Admiral Sir Christopher Craddock, his flag flying in HMS GOOD HOPE, an old armoured cruiser. He was accompanied by MONMOUTH, a smaller cruiser, and some two or three light cruisers. The CANOPUS never caught up with Craddock and on the evening of 1ˢᵗ November, 1914, near Cape Coronel, von Spee came upon the British squadron. The sun was setting behind his ships when he opened fire and our ships were unable to sight the enemy distinctly.

The MONMOUTH and GOOD HOPE were lost with many dead, including J M Pascoe (1912–13), G M Dowding (1911-12), and P S Candy (1912-13). Pascoe and Dowding were Cadets RN, both about the same age, 15¾.

Admiral von Spee swept down to the Horn and made for Port Stanley.

Twenty-four hours before Coronel was fought, an incident took place in Whitehall which altered much. The most progressive Admiral of the steam age and the creator of the Navy which lasted until Taranto 1940, (when the supremacy of the carrier was established), became First Sea Lord. Lord Fisher was one of the hardest taskmasters the Navy has known, he had great intellect and he got things done.

On assuming command, he appreciated that the Falklands could be occupied at any time and he ordered the battlecruisers INVINCIBLE and INFLEXIBLE to Devonport with orders to prepare for the South Atlantic and leave in three days.

There were protests from the yard, a week was demanded. Fisher made a signal signed by the First Lord

(Winston Churchill) ordering the ships to leave in three days. The Dockyard replied that the brick bridges for the boilers and other work would not be finished. Fisher ordered the necessary material to be loaded and the ships to sail if necessary with dockyard mateys aboard. The Admiral Superintendent of the Dockyard came to London to protest. Fisher told him "By the time you get back to the dockyard, the ships must have sailed."

They did … and with dockyard mateys aboard!

If they had sailed later, Fisher would have retired all the senior men concerned with the matter within 24 hours … and they knew it. A delay in sailing of even 24 hours would have lead to the Falklands being occupied by the Germans.

Vice-Admiral Sir Doveton Sturdee commanded the new squadron, which was made up of the two battle cruisers and some light cruisers.

Sub-Lieutenant W H Richardson, RNR, (1907-08), serving in HMS CORNWALL, wrote this account:

'We arrived at Port Stanley, Falklands, on December 7th in company with Vice-Admiral Sturdee and his squadron, and proceeded to coal. On the 8th at 9 am, smoke was observed by the lookout posted on Sapper's Hill, and was soon discovered to be the advance guard of the German Squadron. The alarm was at once given, and all ships prepared for action. At 9.15 the leading ships came within range of the 12 in. guns on board HMS CANOPUS, who fired four salvos over the land, but fell short. By this time our ships, and especially the battle-cruisers, were emitting forth large volumes of smoke, which had the effect of making the

German squadron turn south at full speed. We afterwards gathered from prisoners' statements that they expected to find Port Stanley practically undefended, and received a very rude shock on observing our ships.

'Before leaving the Battle of Coronel a thought for Admiral Craddock who was killed. He had commanded in Bermuda and was highly respected. In his memory, there was founded the Craddock Scholarship by the people of that island. This was specifically for Bermuda boys to be trained in HMS CONWAY, which explains our links and of course the many boys who became Conways were of the highest quality. The arrangement lasted until Cheshire took over the Ship in 1968.

'KENT was the first ship to weigh, and she proceeded for the entrance followed by GLASGOW, CAERNARVON, INFLEXIBLE, INVINCIBLE (Flag) and our ourselves, CORNWALL. The weather conditions were excellent, and by noon our ships were chasing to the southward, at 22 knots. On observing our strength, the German Admiral divided his squadron, the SCHARNHORST and GNEISENAU turning E.S.E., and the three cruisers, DRESDEN, LEIPZIG and NURNBERG continued south. By this time we were overhauling the two former ships rapidly, and at 1 pm the INVINCIBLE and INFLEXIBLE opened fire. Our men were in high spirits, giving vent to the 'Battlesong' with all the force of their lungs. The Germans returned a brisk fire, but the range was too great for their 8.2 guns. Our battle-cruisers soon established hits, and for about fifteen minutes we were most interested spectators. It was indeed a most thrilling experience, the splashes from our 12 in. guns at times completely hiding the enemy. One of our shells practically removed one of the turrets from its ship.

'CORNWALL was now travelling at 24 knots, and having a 'neck and neck' race with the KENT and GLASGOW about one mile ahead of us. At 3 pm, GLASGOW opened fire on their rearmost ship, the LEIPZIG and at 4 pm, we opened fire at 11,000 yards. KENT continued after the two remaining cruisers, later on overhauling and sinking the NURNBERG.

'About this time a signal came from the Admiral, announcing that the SCHARNHORST and GNEISENAU were sunk. CORNWALL was now in the thick of the action, and after about two minutes firing, one of our guns shot away the enemies' fore topmast. A great cheer announced this hit, especially as the German's foremast ensign went with it.

'The firing was returned with great rapidity, and shots were falling all around us. If a gun wouldn't bear for a few minutes, the crew chalked epitaphs on the projectiles, such as 'A Present from Birmingham', 'Here's one from Plymouth', etc.

'By 7 pm, LEIPZIG was badly on fire, and we ceased firing, hoping she would surrender. However, this she refused to do, and we again opened fire. Our lyddite shells sent up great splinters at every hit. At 9 pm. LEIPZIG fired a rocket, and we ceased firing. She was by this time a raging furnace, and only 18 men left alive, out of a crew of 285. GLASGOW and ourselves lowered boats with all speed, and managed to save 16 men between us. The Captain was amongst the last, but unfortunately must have been drowned. At 9.23, LEIPZIG gave a lurch to port, and sank by the head, her starboard propeller just appearing out of water.

'The Germans fought with the greatest possible gallantry, and we all very much regret we were unable to save more. There were no casualties on this ship, which in my opinion, forms the most wonderful feature of this memorable action.

HMS CORNWALL,
Falkland Islands,
December 24th, 1914.'

One of our instructors F H Burfitt (Birdie) had been recalled to the Colours with the outbreak of war and serving as a Chief Petty Officer in HMS KENT wrote this account:

'The German squadron came round the Horn after sinking the GOOD HOPE and MONMOUTH, with the intention of occupying the Falkland Islands, but we just arrived here in time to prevent this. The two Dreadnought Cruisers had started coaling, and the remainder of us were waiting for our colliers to arrive, when we suddenly had the signal to weigh, and then we saw the enemy steaming for the entrance to Stanley Harbour. The old CANOPUS, acting as Guardship, opened fire with her 12 in. guns over the land, but when the Germans saw the tripod masts of our Battle-Cruisers, they were off. They were never so much surprised at anything in their lives, as they didn't know they were with us.

'We, in KENT, were the first ship out, and then came the little GLASGOW, followed by the Dreadnoughts, by which time the enemy were nearly hull down. Our big cruisers soon settled down to the chase, and left us behind. Presently they opened fire, and were replied to by the enemy, whose shells however fell short. We were still out of range, but all the crew collected in the forecastle, and in the rigging, cheering the big ships. Meanwhile GLASGOW had got within range of LEIPZIG, and was barking at him like a little terrier. Now and again she would get a salvo from the enemy, and sheer off out of range, and then close again.

'All this time it was fine sport for us in KENT, but it soon began to get more serious. We sounded action, and started with our bow guns. The shells began to splash and burst close to the ship, and we got hit a couple of times. By this time we had singled out our opponents. We took the NURNBERG, the two Dreadnoughts took the SCHARNHORST, and the GNEISNAU, and the little GLASGOW and CORNWALL, the LEIPZIG. The DRESDEN got away, but we hope to bag her soon.

'Well, we started business then, and we let one another have it hot, and no mistake about it. It took us two hours and forty minutes to finish him, from the time we started. Our casualties were six killed and six wounded. We got the most punishment of all our fleet, and were simply riddled above the water line, though fortunately no serious damage was done.

'The carnage on board the German was awful. All the fore part was on fire, and she began to settle down with a list to starboard. We went in as close as we could with safety, but she would not surrender then, although nearly all her guns were torn out of the deck, and her deck ripped up. She ceased firing for a few minutes, and we did the same, and thought she would haul down her colours; but no, she opened fire again with a couple of her guns. The Captain then ordered us to give her another dose of lyddite, and that fixed her off.

'By that time all who were left alive were gathered on the quarter deck, and I put four lyddite shells into her from my gun. The last one cleared the quarter deck, and ripped the deck open, and one of the prisoners told us afterwards, killed about fifty men. She hauled her colours down then, and one of them waved them in his hand as the ship went down. We picked up seven.

'We have several Old Conways on board, Lieutenant-Commander Redhead, (1887-88), Lieutenant Dunn, (1898-1900), and Mr. Valentime, Midshipman (1910-12).'

So ended the Battle of the Falkland Islands … no Conways were lost.

A strange side light on the affair was the bad blood between the ratings of INVINCIBLE and INFLEXIBLE. Whenever they came together ashore, they fought and had to take shore leave on separate days for the short time their ships remained at Port Stanley after the battle.

So the 1914/18 War started and concluded millions of lives later. After the Battle of the Falkland Islands, ships were seen from time to time, but CONWAY's records do not disclose any events of note.

1933 to 1945

In 1933, Sydney Miller came to the Falklands. He was not a Conway, but his son, R N Miller, (51-53), was born in the Islands in 1936. Sydney Miller was manager of a sheep farm in Roy Cove for 36 years, considered of medium size being of 75,000 acres. Life went on in its own quiet way until the Second World War broke out.

Shortly before war was declared, a German pocket battleship ADMIRAL GRAF SPEE slipped for sea and made for the South Atlantic and Indian oceans. Her job was to act as a commerce cruiser ... that is to capture merchantmen which at that time were still sailing unescorted in these waters.

GRAF SPEE's value lay not in the number of vessels taken or sunk, but in the really vast quantity of resources that were needed to try and contain her menace. As soon as it was known that an enemy raider was in the Southern Oceans measures had to be taken to deal with it. Port Stanley became the supply base for the Royal Navy.

Captain R R Griffith, (1924-27) has written this account. He died on the 28th June, 1983.

'During the 1939-45 war, I was at Stanley from 3rd December, 1939, to 2nd August, 1942, and so at one time I knew many people there. I was Chief Officer of the Fleet Oiler, RFA SAN CASTO. One Falkland Islander has written to me about the middle of each year ever since and sent an annual Christmas card or calendar. Her name is Mrs. L Stacey, she is about 90 now. Her husband, from England, was a PO in one of HM Ships about 60 years ago and was left there to look after Naval Stores and Sheds, also the two oil tanks. So with me being in the tanker we had considerable dealings and our friendship developed. He died at least twenty years ago, without ever coming from the Islands. Mrs Stacey has never been away from there.

'I met five Old Conways who were in the Plate Battle ... with the exception of Commanders (E) Sims and Head (EXETER and ACHILLES) names are forgotten to me, but F E Brooking (Lieutenant in ACHILLES) was on CONWAY with me and a year senior to me. (In addition we know of Captain D H Smith and Sub-Lieutenant H V Williams.)

'One day ACHILLES was to be oiled and we went alongside her. Lieutenant Brooking was on deck. I recognised him and when he came near, I said 'Good morning, Lieutenant B.' and he replied 'Good morning'. No more was said at the time but B. must have wondered how I knew his name, for an hour later there was a knock on my cabin door and there was B. with a query, "How did you know my name?" After that we had a pleasant chat. I wonder if Brooking will remember this incident. The Mr. Miller whom you wrote about was, in those days, well known to me, he was known in those islands as Syd Miller … and myself as Griff of SAN CASTO. Farmers used to visit my ship when they visited Stanley from such places as Goose Green, Darwin, San Carlos, Port Howard, Fox Bay. I still remember their names, but have long since forgotten what they looked like!

'All the Falklands views on TV brought back memories to me and have made me wonder when our trouble with the Argentine is going to end. I well remember that there used to be nothing but trouble with them even when I was an Apprentice. I came home from the Falklands as a passenger in ESPERANCE BAY, and that ship was not allowed to go straight to B. A. without first going to Montevideo to land five of us from the Falklands. We stayed three weeks in Montevideo waiting for the vessel to return to pick us up after loading.'

The River Plate Battle to which Captain Griffith refers was when the cruisers AJAX, ACHILLES and EXETER under Commodore Harwood met the ADMIRAL GRAF SPEE at the mouth of the River Plate. It was not luck … it was reasoned anticipation! In the battle that followed our three ships, though much lighter in weight of shell than their opponent, caused her to seek refuge in the port of Montevideo, Uruguay. She was allowed a limited time to effect repairs and then left but rather than fight she scuttled herself. After that our ships went to Port Stanley to make light repairs and to store.

Commander F W Hunt, MBE, RN, (1936-39), has written this account:

'I first was in the Falklands in 1940 when a Midshipman in HMS HAWKINS. This vessel had become the flagship of Rear Admiral Sir Henry Harwood, victor of the Battle of the River Plate, when he shifted from the AJAX.

'I was in Port Stanley for about a week for rest and recreation and a boiler clean. I enjoyed our stay, but recall that during it the anemometer at the Met station stopped revolving owing to the strength of the wind, an event that had not occurred for more than 50 years.

'The weather was certainly rugged thereabouts as some of the photos I took both at sea and ashore testify.

'In the gunroom of HAWKINS, we had Sub-Lieutenant McVey, (1931-32), with a Master's ticket, but who not long after became a Fleet Air Arm pilot and later an instructor. McVey was the HAWKINS Met Officer and gave me my first practical lesson in the subject in a place where it really mattered.'

1951-1982

Commander Hunt (1936-39) returned to Port Stanley in 1951, being appointed to the JOHN BISCOE.

'I was in charge of the Survey Unit they carried in the ship. The Master was Bill Johnson, who had been Mate and Master of the Falklands Island Company ship, FITZROY.

'We used to take sheep from Port Stanley to Grytviken in South Georgia and whilst there my survey unit was billeted at Leith.

'The work of the JOHN BISCOE involved working round the Falkland Islands. However the Administrators from London used to come to the islands with ideas ahead of reality.

'Thus they decided to put a generator for a proposed freezer plant in Ajax Bay, San Carlos. There was a problem loading in Stanley, but a worse problem befell when it was found that the depth at San Carlos was 1 fathom at high tide, but unfortunately 2½ cables offshore. This was all ascertained after the generator had arrived and found it could not be offloaded.

'A raft was constructed of immense size from 40 gallon drums. The JOHN BRISCOE, with generator aboard, sailed to San Carlos and on arrival on Ajax anchored in three fathoms. The raft came alongside, the idea being for one of the ships boats to tow the raft to the shore and tractors haul on it so that it grounded at high water.

'All went well until the moment for coming ashore; the generator was pulled awkwardly, it rolled off the raft into shallow water and was submerged in due course by the tide. It is probably still there now.

'Commander Hunt at last got the JOHN BISCOE for his exclusive use and he surveyed the Falkland Sound to ensure a clear passage into San Carlos Water, and indeed surveyed San Carlos itself. Survey work of this kind is done by a ship's boat, which in the turbulent waters was always breaking down.

'The only other means at hand was JOHN BISCOE herself and she spent many days taking line soundings until eventually the work was complete. The purpose of surveying San Carlos was on account of the freezer plant at Ajax; eventually they got it working, but it was a waste of time, only one ship ever came to take out 50 tons of meat.

'There were however two benefits. Mr Bonner on whose land the abortive activity took place acquired a very large shed which he could use to store his wool. The second did not occur for nearly thirty years on when the survey work of Commanders Hunt and Penfold (they worked together) was of vital importance for the landing of our troops to take place in San Carlos Water.

'This was unwittingly the first Conway contribution to the Falklands war.'

In 1951, R N Miller, the son of Captain Griffith's friend Syd Miller came to the CONWAY; he is the only islander that I know of who is among our number. The difficulty of becoming an Officer in the MN if a Falklander can be seen by his education. He was born and raised in the Falklands, but for further education, i.e. pre-CONWAY, he had to go to the Grange School in Santiago, Chile. To travel from Stanley in those days meant taking a ship to Montevideo and thence by air to Santiago. For CONWAY, of course, he had to travel from one end of the globe to the other.

On leaving the ship he served his time with Royal Mail and indeed took his tickets with that Company until, having acquired his Master's ticket, he returned home and served aboard the DARWIN, first as Chief Officer and latterly as Master. The DARWIN was used primarily for service within the many islands of the Falklands Group as well as going to Montevideo, South Georgia and the British Antarctic Dependencies.

However, eventually the DARWIN was sold, and as there was no employment about his homeland for this Officer, he joined Fyffes where for some time now he has been Master. During his year as Mate and Master in the Falklands, Captain Miller took note of navigational aids, markers and dangers which contributed to the pilot information for the area.

So we have the second Conway contribution.

THE FALKLANDS WAR
1982
SOUTH GEORGIA

Much of the content of this section was supplied by Brian Lockwood

The first Conways to be involved were Steve Martin, (1970-73), and Brian Lockwood (72-74), on the island of South Georgia.

South Georgia is about 800 miles from Stanley, but is administered from the Falklands. There are no permanent residents, but the British Antarctic Survey has an establishment there, and the head of the BAS acts as legal authority.

In 1982 Steve Martin was that authority, being the Base Commander at King Edward Point. South Georgia was discovered by Captain James Cook in 1775. It is about 100 miles long and 20 wide; to-day there are buildings at Leith and Grytviken, 20 miles apart on the North Coast. It is mountainous, desolate and snow-covered. Sir Ernest Shackleton (Worcester) is buried at Grytviken and visiting ships leave memorials on his tomb.

On March 19th four BAS people were visiting Leith, which should at that time have been completely uninhabited, but they found to their surprise that an Argentine ship was at anchor and about fifty of their men ashore. The Argentine flag was flying from an old building.

Now the BAS people were very suspicious of the Argys because in the month leading up to this landing there had been a visit by a survey yacht, a big ship, IRYZA ALMIRANTI, and an ice breaker. In addition, a reconnaissance aircraft of the Argy air force had been spotted. All this had been reported to Captain Barker, RN, of HMS ENDURANCE and he, it is thought, reported the matter to his superiors.

When the landing at Leith was discovered, the scientists told the Master of the Argentine Vessel BAHIA BUEN SUCESO that neither he nor his men could land without permission and what was worse, they could not shoot reindeer which it was observed they had been doing.

The scientists radioed their news to Steve Martin at Grytviken and he reported to the Governor of the Falkland Islands, who told him to ask the Argentine visitors to report to Grytviken, obtain permission to land and produce passports. This request was given and ignored. The Argys said they had a contract to obtain the scrap metal from the British Embassy in Buenos Aires and in effect refused to have anything to do with Steve Martin and his men.

Twenty-four Royal Marines landed from ENDURANCE on the evening of 24th March and Lieutenant Mills, their Commanding Officer, and Steve Martin considered what should be done. The marines had observers watching Leith, but took no further action on orders from London.

On 25th March an Argentine naval vessel put into Leith and landed troops. It was invasion and the Argys were now the enemy.

On the 3rd April after the Falklands had been occupied, the enemy ship, BAHIA PARAISO signalled Martin using Channel 16 to the effect that the Falklands had surrendered and, if the British would gather on the beach, the enemy would send a party to accept the surrender the following morning.

Steve tried to get a sensible solution, but when it was clear this would not be accomplished and there was going to be trouble, the BAS party took refuge in the Church at Grytviken to await events.

Mills had instructions that if the force against him was overwhelming then put up a token resistance and then surrender. In fact his men shot down a helicopter, heavily damaged the corvette GUERRICO with anti-tank fire so that it had to retire, and caused casualties among the invaders.

It could not last and Lockwood and Martin together with the rest were taken aboard the BAHIA DI BLANCA, which went firstly to Leith and then to Tierra del Fuego. The prisoners were in cabins and the ship went far south to avoid submarines. Martin was questioned by the enemy, but he did not have much to say.

On the mainland they were imprisoned in an old swimming pool until eventually flown home via Montevideo. They were well treated.

Martin's job has been explained. Lockwood is a physicist responsible for maintaining the scientific instruments. He is now back in England having served his BAS time, but Martin is once more down in the cold South.

THE ARGENTINE INVASION
AND OCCUPATION

Sydney Miller

The Falkland Islands Government knew nothing of the coming invasion until 4 pm on the 1st April and the first we, the people, knew about it was by the Government broadcast about 4.30 over the local radio. We were told to stay in our houses and a series of announcements would be made on the hour right through the night. The invaders had come into Port William, the outer harbour, in the evening of the 1st but did not start coming ashore until the early hours of the 2nd.

The eighty Royal Marines had moved overnight from their quarters at Moody Brook, at the head of Stanley harbour. Their section nearest the landing beaches caused quite heavy casualties with mortar shells, sinking one landing craft full of troops before it reached the beach and plastering another as it was coming on to the beach causing several more casualties. The marines then withdrew to the approach to the town and later when the first of the Argentine light tanks came up the airport road, they put another mortar shell into the leading machine which killed its crew and temporarily blocked the road. The marines being so few against, by that time, some 2,000 enemy troops, withdrew to Government House. Finally, when the outcome was obviously quite hopeless for them to be in any way effective, they were told to surrender by the Governor. It is noteworthy that not a single marine had as much as a scratch on the body, but their fire had been very effective against the invaders.

We just stayed put in our houses listening to the, by then, half-hourly broadcasts from Government House. After it was all over, we were again told to stay put by the Argentines for the rest of that day. The town by then was very full of both troops and vehicles, from huge armoured troop carriers, tanks and trucks down to motor cycles. We ventured out when we had to go to the shops or post office etc., but the Argentine troops were completely astonished when no Islander would give them as much as a good morning. They had been filled with propaganda before they left that most of the population was thirsting to become Argentine … they were a very puzzled lot of troops. And so it went on for two and a half months … no conversation connection with the invaders though Islanders meeting in the streets would be full of conversation to each other. We were angry when they started to install heavy and anti-aircraft guns throughout the town in peoples' gardens and grounds, and we were even more angry when their two successive Red Cross ships came in, ostensibly to collect casualties and corpses, but spent several hours unloading more troops, ammunition and finally a stock of Exocet missiles, one of which hit HMS Glamorgan just before the end and caused many casualties. The Royal

Navy came in most nights, off Port Harriet, and plastered the Argentine positions in the hills west of the town. Their 4.5 shelling was very accurate, though two successive shells just before the end landed a little short and killed three women in the house where they were sheltering.

When the nightly naval bombardment started up, usually about 10.30 pm, my wife and I would immediately look up and say 'The Navy's here' and, probably unintelligently, go outside and watch the shells bursting on the Argy positions.

And so it went on but no Islander right from the first day had any doubt at all that the old country would respond and once they were ashore at Port San Carlos, where my second son was station manager (30,000 sheep there), we knew we would not have many days to wait, and so it happened. The Argy troops really did not have much chance against British troops so professional and well trained and so fit and tough. The Argentine command had heavily mined the beaches where they had originally come ashore, being quite sure the British would land there, for the terrain between Stanley and the San Carlos area is wet, with soft peaty ground. It was winter time of course, though Falkland Island winters are never as severe as your winters can be in Britain, in spite of the rubbish that so many reporters wrote about the savage cold weather. However, the Argy calculations were wrong and the Paras, the Royal Marines and the rest came the hard way, on foot overland, and in a very short time too. I would think those British troops must be the very best trained and toughest troops in the world … to us they were magnificent.

THE TASK FORCE

On 31st March the British Government realised an invasion was to take place and it decided as a matter of political will that if this did happen the islands would be recaptured by force.

The Task Force consisted of 114 ships of which only 37 were RN and 77 MN, being divided into 25 RFA and 52 from Trade.

I had never realised and I suspect that there are many who do not realise the quite enormous contribution of the MN to the enterprise. Apart from a few ships of renown or disaster very little has been said of the ships of the MN yet they were there overwhelmingly in the majority, acting not just as supply vessels, but as aircraft carriers, minesweepers, and in the case of NORLAND leading the Royal Navy to the landing place at San Carlos.

The Merchant Navy was first in and last out.

When the Falklands were occupied, the Prime Minister set up a small Committee of Cabinet Ministers and the Chief of Defence Staff (CDS) with herself as Chairman.

The official name was 'Defence and Overseas Policy Committee, Sub Committee on the South Atlantic and Falkland Islands (OD(SA))', but everyone called it the War Cabinet for that is what it was.

The Ministers were the Secretaries of State for Home, Foreign and Defence Affairs, together with the Paymaster General. The War Cabinet was the body that made the key political, diplomatic and military decisions during the Falklands war. The CDS had to provide military information and advice which he gathered from the Heads of the Services, the views of his own Commander-in-Chief and the Operational Commanders in the South Atlantic.

In fact the recapture of the Islands was largely a Navy command responsibility because Rear Admiral Woodhouse was in command of the ships at sea, and on land the commander Major General Moore was a Royal Marine Officer.

The military control was directed by the overall commander at Northwood, Admiral Sir John Fieldhouse.

There was one Officer appointed to give to Admiral Sir Terence Lewin (CDS) the digested military information and in such form that it would be understandable to the War Cabinet. The same Officer would receive from CDS the decisions of the War Cabinet and would be required to put them into the form of an operational directive, which he would then pass to Admiral Fieldhouse at Northwood.

This Officer, called Assistant Chief of Defence Staff (Operations), was Vice-Admiral D W Brown (1941-45), the most senior serving RN Officer concerned with the Falklands War so far as I am aware from CONWAY, WORCESTER and Pangbourne.

His job was difficult and complex and to quote Admiral Brown.

"The job was really one of politico/military interface, presentation of the military view, speed/time/distance constraints, information flow, operational directives to Special Forces, trouble-shooting, and perhaps the most complex of all was the Rules of Engagement. The latter was an interpretation of whether HM Government was escalating, retaining the status quo, or de-escalating, and in case specific rules had to be signalled to Commanding Officers of HM Ships and Aircraft, giving clear and positive guidance as to what could or could not be done".

An example of the work would be putting forward an assessment of the position with regard to the enemy cruiser, GENERAL BELGRANO, and eventually giving the directive that she should be attacked in certain circumstances.

Admiral Brown's job lasted throughout the campaign; it was very hard work occupying all hours. It is a matter of great pride that the planners got it right. For by the 5th April, the Task Force sailed. Afterwards they said there were no contingency plans, but whether or not there were, it is worth looking at the work needed to assemble the Task Force.

The son of a Conway, a Captain in the Royal Irish Rangers, was taken from Honduras where he had just landed with his company of troops and flown back home for special training in the wilds of Wales, one month before the invasion.

On 31st March CDS was in New Zealand. The Royal Navy had many people either on Easter leave or about to go on it. The many ships of the Merchant Navy likely to be required were at Sea. CANBERRA was approaching Gibraltar, UGANDA was cruising in the Med, QUEEN ELIZABETH II was cruising the Atlantic towards home, the many ferries were busy with the holiday trade and some ships laid up.

The Royal Fleet Auxiliary were scattered about the oceans and Captain C G Butterworth (1941-43), Marine Superintendent of RFA, was working overtime to get his 25 ships provisioned and away.

On 29th March, FORT AUSTIN at Gibraltar was told she was being sent to Falklands. A few days later TIDESPRING then on her way to join the Chilean Navy was diverted to Ascension Island and the sale cancelled. SIR GALAHAD and SIR GERAINT were loading in Plymouth, SIR TRISTAN would arrive later from Canada.

The first elements of the Task Force sailed on 5th April, the second a day later. They made their way relatively slowly to Ascension Island. The reasons for this were several. It was hoped that this display of arms would make the enemy more amenable to negotiate and settlement, but this required time. It was important that fuel be conserved ('consumption of fuel varies as the speed squared' … Charles Nicholls. As a matter of interest, Charles Nicholls had been Chief Engineer in the MN and was for many years instructor of engineering in HMS CONWAY. He had the superb gift of being able to teach and so successfully that his expressions, such as the one cited, are never forgotten by Conways.

It gave time for the various elements to be assembled, and varied they were, bearing in mind that the vast majority of the ships were Merchantmen.

We are reporting on the doings of our people so let these accounts speak for themselves with reference to their ships.

QUEEN ELIZABETH II

R W Warwick (1956-57), Chief Officer of the Queen Elizabeth II kept a diary.

4 May 1982

Ship requisitioned by MOD on arrival alongside berth at 0200 hrs. Work commenced to prepare ship for military use. Quarter deck forward extended over capstan machinery to provide helicopter landing platform. Upper deck lido cut off in line with aft end of Q4 bar ... quarter deck extended right over both pools. Inside of pools used as main foundation for deck to provide landing for two helicopters.

Independent radio room being fitted in barn behind bridge. Pipework being fitted at starboard midship baggage entrance on two deck to enable refueling to be carried out at sea. Pictures and valuable items being removed from ship. Also many chairs and all casino equipment. All plants and shrubs removed. China, glass and silverware collected up and stowed.

Hardboard being laid over all carpets, in public rooms and passageways, on stairways and some cabins. All concessionaire and unnecessary crew laid off. Military equipment, food stores being loaded on board plus extra life-jackets, life-rafts and safety appliances.

9 May

Commenced loading ammunition in No 1 hold. Ammunition in containers also loaded on sports deck forward of funnel. Landrovers, trailers, helicopter fuel and rations loaded on open decks aft on raised boatdeck and what's left of upper deck.

12 May

The embarkation of troops commenced at 0545 hrs ... their regimental bands on hand to play them aboard.

Visit to the ship by Lord Matthews. Various military

leaders, the Lord Mayor of Southampton, also John Nott, Minister of Defence, who toured the bridge and spoke to the troops.

Despite technical problems and high winds the ship put to sea on schedule leaving berth at 1603 hrs. Thousands on hand to see her sail. When off Portsmouth, two Sea King helicopters landed on after flight deck and were stowed. They are part of the 825 Squadron now on board. A meeting was held in the wardroom during the evening and the now resident Naval Party were elected temporary members.

13 May

Boat drill was held at 1030 for the 3,000 embarked troops. Some rearranging was necessary as we had never had to cope with so many people before. All lifeboats were swung out to embarkation level during the morning.

During the afternoon a medical emergency, a young soldier with appendicitis. He was promptly flown by helicopter to Culdrose along with another with an injured foot. At 1836, RFA Grey Rover approached for a replenishment at sea exercise. The hose was successfully connected up by 1900 and the lines tested.

At 2035 the helicopter returned and we proceeded southerly avoiding the main shipping lanes.

14 May

Physical exercises began at 0650. Every unit on board has a time slot for jogging. All day they go round and round the boat deck ... the noise is quite incredible. Some are fully kitted out with enormous ruck-sacks, shovels and rifles. Troops on board are 5th Infantry Brigade from the Welsh Guards, Scots Guards and the Duke of Edinburgh's Own Gurkha Rifles.

15 May

Military exercises started today with firing practice with live ammunition. Bags of garbage were used as targets. Some 29 tons of ammunition was put on board for practice use on the way south. Every part of the ship is in use for some form of training.

16 May

The Captain held a church service in the theatre … it was almost full … while firing practice continues all morning from the fore and after decks. Assault stations started for the troops.

17 May

The troops now wear boots for jogging so their feet don't become soft. Only trouble in that it is playing havoc with the decks … the caulking is lifting out all over the place!

18 May

Arrived at Freetown, 1000 hours. Our inaugural call at this port, but no ceremony. All the official formalities were waived and there was no shore leave. Only a handful of people were allowed on board. Fuel oil and water were taken on board and a few bags of potatoes. The ship put to sea at 2230.

19 May

The ship is now 'blacked out' at night … every window and porthole is covered so the ship cannot be seen at night. Even the navigation lights and radars are put off. It is unpleasant not waking up to the morning sunlight.

The ship crossed the line today. We have been building a swimming pool on the foredeck and a ceremony was duly held organised by the Navy. All hands given time off to attend. Night flying exercises in the evening.

20 May

At 1445 rendezvous with HMS DUMBARTON CASTLE. Helicopter transfer of personnel and equipment. Ascension Island in sight. Blackout from 1840 hours.

21 May

At 0800 commenced taking on more stores and troops by helicopter from Ascension Island. Ship steamed about 30 miles off the island. Our two Sea Kings used, plus some from the RAF base and also a Chinook. Mail was sent off and also taken on board for us and for others near the Falklands. An estimated 10 tons of mail was taken on board. Some mail was posted to the BFPO address on the 17th May and received here today. During the night there was a rendezvous with the SS Atlantic Causeway.

22 May

Military lookouts are now posted on the bridge wings and near the funnel from dawn to darkness. All soldiers are armed with rifles.

Commenced the erection of a platform to hold the mounting of a .5 Browning machine gun on each bridge wing. Job involves more drilling and welding. Rendezvous with ATLANTIC CAUSEWAY at 0710. Helicopter transfers until 1040 hours.

Major-General J J Moore, CB, OBE, MC, Commander Land Forces and his staff joined yesterday. Brigadier M J A Wilson is the Commander of the 5th Infantry Brigade (he joined at Southampton). Also on board is Linda Kitson, who has been commissioned by the Imperial War Museum and Fleet Air Arm to draw.

23 May

The sea has been rippled all day with exceptionally good visibility and a clear horizon. There are scattered fair weather cumulus, which can be seen clearly right down to the horizon. There were no flying exercises today ... fuel must be conserved. Church was held in the cinema but the attendance was only a third of last week's.

At lunchtime the wardroom invited all the women employed in the ship up for drinks. There are about 30 on board.

24 May

Ship set course towards South Georgia. Browning machine guns now operative on the Bridge wings and firing exercises carried. Gun has a capability of firing one thousand rounds per minute.

No 5 raft launching davit fall wire damaged by practice gunfire and had to be replaced. Bullet holes made in forward rails ... strong protests made at 15.15 meeting.

25 May

Very heavy rain squalls early in the morning did not inhibit the unceasing physical exercises ... soldiers in full battle kit drenched to the skin in the cold rain, continued to run around the deck. Fog patches in the evening. There have been many requests for lifejackets from the crew; many have also asked for training exercises on lifeboats and raft launching. Crew have to be ordered to this training in normal circumstances and usually every excuse imaginable is used to avoid doing so! Engineer officers have been instructed to take an active interest in the boats that they are assigned to — we wish this had happened twelve years ago!

26 May

It is getting cold now with temperatures near zero. Distribution of personal ammunition continues ... constant stream of trucks up and down the alleyways from the forward holds are causing the inevitable damage to bulkheads and the floor protection.

Our destination, which hitherto has been variable and uncertain, is now becoming clearer. We are heading for South Georgia, and hope to rendezvous with HMS ANTRIM and later with the merchant ships CANBERRA and NORLAND.

The loss of the ATLANTIC CONVEYOR has cast a cloud over the ship and more of the ship's company are becoming increasingly aware of the reality of the situation that we have found ourselves in.

A few hours spent with the military today to try and plan how we will discharge the troops, equipment and stores. The ship has maintained radio silence since passing Ascension Island; not being in communication with the other ships so a positive plan c cannot be formulated. Four lifeboats (Hardings) have been stripped of their netting so they can be used for transporting the troops or stores.

The sailors will lay in tomorrow as they may well have to work all night. The helicopters can fly at night from QE II, but it is not known if they can operate from the CANBERRA and NORLAND. It was hoped that we would also meet RFA STROMNESS, but she has obviously been deployed elsewhere in view of the increasing losses to our fleet.

27 May

Some of the icebergs are most spectacular ... one looks like the white cliffs of Dover and another like a cathedral spire looming up from the sea. There are dozens around. Every now and again the mist closes in and navigation is tricky.

Rendezvous with HMS Antrim in the forenoon, General Moore and his staff transferred. Two of our boats launched to transfer the soldiers and stores, the General went by helicopter. The sea was calm, but the swell was several feet high. Unfortunately one soldier got his leg trapped between the launch and ANTRIM and broke it badly. He was returned to our hospital by the helicopter.

Our boats were recovered without difficulty; considerable stress, however, was put on the falls as the weight came on them suddenly caused by the swell wave. Stress was transmitted up to the davit level and caused a fracture in the bedding of the after unit No 11.

The ship proceeded to and anchored in Cumberland Bay East near the old whaling station of Grytviken ... the place where the scrap metal merchants landed. Soon after our arrival, Captain Barker of HMS ENDURANCE, and the Senior Naval Officer, Captain C Burne, of the CANBERRA came on board to meet with Captain James RN, (the Senior RN Liaison Officer on board), and the Brigadier remaining on board, of General Moore's staff.

This meeting was to agree on a plan of how to disembark the troops and discharge the cargo. Our plans had been to commence the cargo right away and start disembarking troops at first light in the morning. As it would take about 48 hours to discharge the cargo, there seemed little point in moving the troops overnight.

This was, however, contrary to the thoughts of the Senior Naval Officer who had of course also been considering and making plans before our arrival. The SNO was of the opinion that the troops should also move right away. It was an interesting experience to be witness to the battle of words that ensued … men of strong personality and character expressing their respective views in the firmest and calmest way. Eventually agreement was reached and about 700 troops disembarked overnight commencing at 2145 hours for transfer to CANBERRA and NORLAND. Requisitioned British trawlers, fitted out with mine sweeping equipment, had arrived at the island the day before and were used for the transfer. Despite the late hour the soldiers seemed to be in good spirit. The amount of kit they each had to carry was quite incredible and it was difficult to imagine that they would be able to travel with such a load for long periods over rough terrain.

The trawlers came alongside with difficulty … it was a dark night and the minimum of lights was used. No doubt some paint has been scoured off the hull. A start was made on the discharge of number 1 hatch, but eventually had to be abandoned until daylight … the flair of the bow being difficult to negotiate in the darkness.

28 May
Our first sight of the Cumberland Bay came with the dawn. Snow capped mountains leading down to glaciers flowing into the sea and small icebergs scattered about the bay.

Discharge of the troops and stores commenced again at 0800. The helicopters departed for the last time and remained on board the CANBERRA.

29 May

The snow started to fall at 0400 and by daybreak it had settled and everywhere was covered by a couple of inches. Visibility was negligible so it was most fortunate that the two helicopters had transferred the previous day. Nevertheless more than 100 tons of stores have yet to go.

This is loaded onto the trawlers for the transfer to STROMNESS which arrived shortly before noon, and a launch was next ashore to collect some of the marines based at Grytviken and bring them on board for lunch. The Captain in charge took the opportunity of showing some of us around the old whaling station … where the Falklands crisis really began.

Nearby was the Argentine submarine SANTE FE … she was sunk though the conning tower was still above the surface. Most of the timber buildings were in a derelict state. The church, in contrast, was in good condition and had been looked after by various visitors in 20 years since the station was closed.

One of the Officers even got touching music out of the old organ. Near the shore line overlooking a forlorn looking wooden hulk was the cemetery. The most recent grave was that of an Officer from the SANTE FE, killed in action. Shackleton's grave stood proud of all others and was decorated at the base with crested shields of visiting ships.

Some of us came away with harpoon heads, the most that anyone is permitted to remove. Our nursing sister, Wendy Marshall, who had the honour of being the only girl on the island, was able to bring a large piece of whale bone back on board for the ships doctor! It was a most interesting expedition. As a matter of interest, RWW, the author of this diary was unaware that Cindy Buxton and Annie Price were doing research on the south coast of the island.

We returned to our ship with about thirty young marines who were based at Grytviken. They were anxious to get on board the ship for a few hours … which, in turn, was also an unexpected change of routine for them. Importantly we also carried mail … a thing they had not received for some weeks. The embarkation took place during the afternoon of some 640 survivors of HMS ARDENT, COVENTRY and ANTELOPE.

The barometer was falling steadily throughout the day and towards mid-afternoon it became apparent that the weather was giving cause for concern as the wind force increased. The trawlers had difficulty staying alongside with safety. Our port gangway and pontoon were damaged beyond further use.

Eventually discharging had to be abandoned. The anchor was weighed and a lee formed to allow a trawler to come alongside and take off the remaining personnel. Meanwhile, during the afternoon a report was received that a tanker, the BRITISH WYE, had been under attack. An Argentine aircraft had dropped bombs, but fortunately they all missed. The incident was a particular cause for concern as the tanker was a considerable distance from the mainland and many miles north of the islands.

When QE2 cleared Cumberland Bay, an easterly course was set to endeavour to reduce our vulnerability to this threat. So, at the end of the day we put to sea with about 60 tons of ammunition still on board.

30 May
Church service at 1100 held by Captain Jackson with lesson and special prayers read by Captain James. The weather is bad, rough sea and heavy swells.

31 May

Early call to deal with spillage of acid on two deck aft. It was necessary to evacuate many of the cabins in the area which was unfortunate as I imagine that would be the last thing that survivors would want.

1 June

We are heading northerly towards Ascension. The stock of fuel is getting low. Rendezvous with the BAYLEAF in the afternoon, but the weather is too bad to carry out the RAS (Replenishment at Sea).

2 June

Early morning rendezvous with the BAYLEAF. The hose was coupled up successfully shortly after 0800 and oil was pumped aboard throughout the day. The sea is still rough and great strain was put on the hose … it was nearly horizontal at times.

3 June

Today, we received the news that we would proceed directly to Southampton after our rendezvous off Ascension tomorrow. This news was received with very mixed emotions. Many of the crew are emotionally geared up to spending at least two months away and are totally unprepared for returning home so soon. A lot don't feel they have achieved enough to the general cause and would wish to see us in what they consider a more active role.

It is unfortunate because this ship has achieved something which would not otherwise have been possible and everyone on board is part of that.

4 June

During the afternoon we had a rendezvous with the HMS DUMBARTON CASTLE. She is stationed on the starboard bow and, using an RAF Sea King helicopter from Ascension, we transferred about 25 tons of ammunition and mail. The ammunition is to be put aboard another ship detailed for the islands. We had good weather conditions so the operation was carried out swiftly. A couple of the more seriously injured soldiers were also taken off.

5 June

A group of survivors of one of the ships has decided to build a swimming pool on the afterdeck. The survivors all look after their own accommodation and some of them do odd jobs during the morning. Apart from that they are more or less free to do as they please. Sports are arranged every day so inter-ship competition is kept alive.

6 June

Today the Captain told us that the ship was to be handed back to the owners and that it is likely to be in refit until August 14. My own theory was that we would be back in service for the 3rd July cruise!

8 June

The survivors held a Miss QE2 competition … there were five entries and a sailor with a beard won!

9 June

News is gradually filtering through about our arrival arrangements. We will be met in the Solent by the Queen Mother on the Royal Yacht.

R.W.W.

On Saturday 12th June Queen Elizabeth II arrived home, perhaps one of her most important services carried out on the voyage home was cheering up the survivors who had seen friends lost in horrible circumstances, many survivors were injured but they returned as victors.

The Royal Yacht Britannia met QE II, along with a vast number of small crafts and yachts. 6000 friends and relatives manned the quay, the bands played, the crowds cheered the troops and survivors, and the crew of the QE II went quietly about their business to prepare for the refit.

APPOINTED AND DISAPPOINTED

It will be recalled that Commander Hunt and Captain Miller made a contribution to the Survey of the Falklands. That was a bonus contribution years before the war, as indeed was the really outstanding work of Major Southby-Tailyour RM, who though Pangbourne, is by temperament also a Conway. His Greenwich Naval report is said to contain 'This Officer prefers fighting to writing and is not recommended for further staff training at this establishment'. In 1978 whilst on duty at the Falklands, he mapped and charted every major bay and inlet in the islands and filled 126 pages of notebooks with key navigational data.

For the Falklands War his survey work was invaluable. Indeed there was no other in existence, but the Admiralty had not been interested. They had not even got a copy. Now it was required and the Major told them "If you want my work you must take me." To their credit they did. The Officers responsible for finally selecting the landing place at San

Carlos were Commodore Clapp and Brigadier Thompson. Major Southby-Tailyour was able to point out to them the nautical/amphibious advantages/disadvantages of the many different options through his personal knowledge and able to steer them towards the likely landing places.

Many of our people in the Reserve volunteered for service, but the RN did tremendously well using its own resources and of course those of the MN. In fact only a few specialists were recalled for duty. Those who volunteered and who perhaps had reasonable prospects of service included Captain D T Smith, RN, (41-43). Some years ago he had been Commodore Amphibious Warfare.

Yet another was Captain R N Miller, who it will be recalled has great experience in navigating the seas, sounds and inlets about his homeland, and was in truth the nearest equivalent to a Falkland Islands Pilot that one can get. Both these Officers were frustrated at not being required.

Captain A P Woodhead, RN, (1954-56), spent the war in HMS HERMES.

He was pulled back from leave and appointed Chief of Staff to the Task Force Commander, Rear-Admiral Woodhouse, following preparatory work at home.

"I flew down in mid-April to join the Flagship HERMES in Ascension."

Such was the enormous amount of work of planning the landing and all that goes with it that in order to make the best use of available staff expertise, Woodhead and another Officer stood watch and watch as Group Warfare Officer concentrating on the daily running of the Task Group which at any time might number up to 80 ships. The RN/MN liaison worked extremely well over the whole crisis period.

The conditions were as bad as seamen can imagine, very cold, very rough, no fresh milk or vegetables, in fact a fair amount of discomfort.

Captain Woodhead does not mention it, but one has heard that when weather permitted, the flight deck was in use 24 hours of the day. The HERMES would move in and out of range of enemy aircraft from the mainland … though usually in range of aircraft operating from Port Stanley Airport. In fact, the risk of attack was minimised by our action against that field which, though operational to the last night of the war, could not after the first few days of our offensive launch aircraft capable of crippling the HERMES. The greatest danger to our surface ships was thought to be the submarine, but the Argentine force never proved to be a serious menace, owing to our defensive action.

The ships of the Task Force were closed up for battle at action stations when within range of the enemy and the ships' company had to sleep dressed in the corridors and flats ready for action.

Captain Woodhead said:

"The young sailors performed beyond all expectations in this wild environment and the youth of today, disparaged by so many for so long, showed the same guts and commitment as any previous generation."

This tribute is singular because it has been made before by an Officer in the same position as Captain Woodhead.

That Officer was virtually the founder of the Conway, his name Captain W Mendes, RN, and he planned at sea, when Flag Captain to the Commander of the British Fleet, the successful landing of the British Army on the shores of Crimea in 1854.

Unfortunately, Captain Woodhead is not able to tell us more of his job.

NORLAND
Leads the Way

When it came to the landing, it was the Merchant Ship NORLAND that led the way. Her Chief Officer was R B Lough, (1961-63), and here is his account:

NORLAND was launched in Bremerhaven in 1973 at the A G Wesser shipyard and was commissioned in June 1974 on North Sea Ferries Hull to Rotterdam service. She was designed to carry 1,200 passengers and approximately 100 freight units on a 12 hour overnight crossing of the North Sea.

The NORLAND (12,988 gross tons) is one of the larger North Sea Ferries and thus by definition totally unsuitable for the seas around the Falklands.

On April 17th she was requisitioned by the Ministry of Defence to be converted to carry troops south to the Falkland Islands. The main problems to be overcome to enable the ship to go south were:

1. The ship's fuel capacity had to be increased. In normal service across the North Sea the ship could be refuelled every day if necessary, therefore the ship was designed to carry only 530 tonnes of oil. To overcome this, the ship's ballast tanks which had a capacity of 1,000 tonnes had to be cleaned and converted to carry fuel. When this was done it gave the ship a range of 32 days steaming which would

enable her to sail direct from Portsmouth to the Falklands without refuelling.

2. Fresh water capacity had to be increased. This was done by installing a desalination plant to convert sea water to fresh. As the ship's main tank capacity was only 600 tonnes, 9 rubber pillow tanks were installed on F deck with a capacity of 400 tonnes, to give a total capacity of 1,000 tonnes.

3. Store rooms for food were not large enough. NORLAND was contracted to support 1000 men for 60 days at sea, so enough food had to be loaded into the ship to feed them. This was achieved by loading 10 refrigerated and 30 ordinary containers on the car decks.

4. The ship had to be fitted with RAS Point (Replenishment at Sea) to enable her to refuel and water at sea from the RFA tankers which were stationed on the route south from UK to Falklands.

5. The ship had to be fitted with two Sea King helicopter decks, one aft and one amidships, to enable us to work helicopters.

This work was done in Hull and Portsmouth and was completed in nine days.

The NORLAND had on board in addition to the Ship's Officers, Officers and men of the Royal Navy. Their job was in effect to make the Merchant Navy part of the Royal Navy, but of course no Master worth his salt would allow some Brass Hat to push him around his own Bridge, especially as the only people to have seen any real war service before were some of the MN Masters.

The job required the greatest of tact, and it worked, though those MN Officers with RNR Commissions had an advantage in explaining the ways of the RN to their colleagues. There is still the old-fashioned view amongst some MN Officers that the RN is a toffee-nosed lot, and of course it is generally accepted that they don't do much sea time. Great credit is due to RN Liaison Officers for doing this extraordinarily difficult job so well.

The NORLAND got on well with their RN party and after a few days for adjustment both sides worked well together and became a ship with one Master and crew which included the RN specialists.

On April 26th 1982, NORLAND loaded the 2nd Battalion, The Parachute Regiment, and sailed for the Falkland Islands. We arrived at Ascension Island on May 17th, having called at Freetown, Sierra Leone, for fuel and water, and sailed on the evening of May 7th to join the Task Force. We joined up with CANBERRA, HMS FEARLESS, HMS INTREPID, ATLANTIC CONVEYOR, EUROPIC FERRY, STROMNESS and ELK, plus the escorts HMS ARDENT and ARGONAUT on May 10th and proceeded South. On May 16th, we joined the second part of the Assault Group at an ocean rendezvous … PEARLEAF, PLUMLEAF, BRITISH LANCE, SIR GALAHAD, SIR TRISTAM, SIR GERAINT, SIR PERCIVAL, FORT TORONTO and the destroyer HMS ANTRIM

On May 18th, the whole Fleet met up with Admiral Woodhouse's HERMES Task Force and we were poised for the assault.

Major Southby-Taylor flew from FEARLESS to NORLAND to brief Chief Officer Lough for he was to be the Pilot into San Carlos.

On the night of May 20/21st, HMS PLYMOUTH escorted HMS INTREPID, HMS FERARLESS and NORLAND, followed by CANBERRA, STROMNESS, EUROPIC FERRY and FORT AUSTIN into the Falkland Sound.

NORLAND made her way into the Falkland Sound between the two great islands of East and West Falkland and then altered to port between the Headlands of Fanning Head and Chancho Point. Once past, the ships moved to the mouth of San Carlos Water, NORLAND leading all the way until anchoring.

FEARLESS, INTREPID and NORLAND close to Chancho Point and we disembarked the troops (2nd Parachute Regiment) through the shell doors into LCUs. They had great difficulty 'in getting out' with a heavy rise and fall. After the LCUs had gone in, NORLAND weighed anchor and was the first ship to enter San Carlos Water. We anchored at Doctor's Point and during the next three hours the whole of the landing fleet entered and anchored. As the sun rose, we found ourselves surrounded by the hills of the Falkland Islands. It was the end of our first journey, twenty five days out from Portsmouth. NORLAND led in case the channels were mined, as she was considered to be the most expendable of the several ships.

The beachhead at San Carlos had a hard time during the next four days with frequent bombing attacks from Skyhawk and Mirage jets. HMS ARDENT and HMS ANTELOPE were sunk and a lot of other ships damaged. NORLAND had one near miss on 24th May when two 500 pound bombs landed close alongside her.

ANTELOPE had escorted NORLAND on our second entry into San Carlos on the morning of May 23rd. Due to a delay in detaching us from the HERMES battle group the night before, we had to make the entry in daylight. With still twelve miles to run to the 'safety' of Bomb Alley, Air Raid Warning Red was called with two Mirage aircraft up Falkland Sound. Fortunately for us they were seen off by two Sea Harriers sent on CAP from INVINCIBLE. ANTELOPE saw us safely to anchor, then took up her position covering the entrance to the bay. A few hours later she was hit by two bombs dropped by two Skyhawks right alongside us and as you know one of them exploded while being defused later that night.

The ship's company of ANTELOPE was taken aboard NORLAND and delivered to QE II in South Georgia.

The link that developed has not been lost. The main bar on NORLAND has been renamed the Antelope Bar and was opened by Nick Tobin, Captain of ANTELOPE, when the ship came back into service. It contains a showcase with all the mementoes of the Falklands Campaign plus a very fine oil painting based on the photograph..

NORLAND anchored in Grytviken Harbour, South Georgia on the evening of May 27th. QE II arrived at 2200 and we started cross decking the 7th Gurhka Rifles with their equipment plus the 16th Field Ambulance. We sailed on the evening of May 28th for the Falklands and entered San Carlos Water again. June 1st we landed the Gurkhas. The following day we loaded 500 prisoners and then sailed to wait offshore with HERMES group.

On June 7th we re-entered San Carlos Water and loaded another 500 prisoners. We sailed again under cover of darkness to replenish with fuel and water offshore before heading off to Montevideo to repatriate the prisoners.

We arrived at Montevideo on June 12th, discharged the prisoners and sailed on the morning of June 13th for the Falklands.

NORLAND entered San Carlos Water for the fifth time on June 17th and loaded 1,000 prisoners which had been brought from Fox Bay in the INTREPID. We sailed 53 miles in daylight on June 18th from San Carlos to Port Stanley, arriving at 1712 that evening, and 14,960 miles since sailing from Portsmouth.

We spent the night loading another 1,000 prisoners and sailed the following morning with 2,000 prisoners on board to Puerto Madryn in Argentina. These were discharged on June 21st and the ship returned to Port Stanley, arriving on June 23rd.

The survivors of the 2nd and 3rd Battalions of the Parachute Regiment embarked on June 24th and the ship sailed for Ascension Island on June 25th. She arrived there on 5th July and disembarked the Paras to fly home. NORLAND then loaded the Queen's Own Highlanders plus 15 Falkland Islanders and re-stored for the journey back to the Falklands. She sailed for Port Stanley on July 9th in her new role as a South Atlantic ferry.

The GEESTPORT

The story of a typical Merchantman engaged in the Falklands is that of the GEESTPORT. Her Master, Captain G de Ferry Foster, (1954-56), wrote his memoirs.

In early May, this ship was chartered by DOT to act as a forward support ship to the Royal Navy. We duly sailed from Avonmouth to Portsmouth RN Dockyard and had several modifications carried out. Stump masts were fitted to the ship so that stores could be transferred between ships while underway and also so that refuelling could take place at sea. A helicopter flight deck or 'Vertrep deck' was built so that stores and personnel could be transferred by helicopter.

After loading Naval stores, we sailed from Portsmouth. We carried out a dummy RAS off Portland to test the modifications fitted at Portsmouth, and then proceeded to the South Atlantic via Ascension, then a devious route south, which, for the last two days before arriving at our first destination in the Total Exclusion Zone, took us through very heavy concentrations of icebergs, never less than fifty-seven within a twelve mile radius of the ship. The icebergs showed up well on the radar and so caused no problems apart from the fact that times it was hard to find a way through them. The main difficulty was with growlers and bergy bits which do not show up, and these together with the atrocious weather and the constant thought that an Argy might be about … well slightly worrying … dead slow ahead and no sleep for the Old Man.

We were in the Total Exclusion Zone for just under three months and during that time visited all (or most) of the famous places. During the period we did a total of 58 stores transfers to HM Ships, RFAs, RAF units and Army units ashore, and also to STUFTS, (ships taken up from trade). Stores transfers took place by boat, helicopter and alongside, ship to ship.

After a final transfer with INVINCIBLE, we left the area on the 4th August and arrived back at Portsmouth on 19th August … a non-stop, flat-out passage at an average speed of 20.02 knots.

As we were the 43rd ship back we expected to arrive back as quietly as we had left, but the Navy gave us a welcome that I will never forget. My wife and children were invited to accompany the Port Captain in his launch to escort us in. The decks of all HM ships and shore establishments were manned and gave us three cheers as we passed. The sight of HERMES flight deck manned for us is something I will never forget.

And so home on leave. On 12th October I was one of five Masters to be invited to the City of London salute to the Task Force and had the honour of representing my ship at a reception at the Mansion House and lunch at the Guildhall … another day to remember.

The EUROPIC FERRY

Captain W J C Clarke, (1959-62), was Master of the EUROPIC FERRY, his Chief Officer was Norman Bamford, (1961-63), and Second Officer A G Burns, (1948-50). He also had with the troops embarked Staff Sergeant R L Peacock, (1969-71), of RAOC Tideworth.

Captain Clarke writes:

The ship was requisitioned by the Secretary of State for Trade on the 19th April, for service with the South Atlantic Task Force. During the next three days she was modified in Southampton to carry out her new role, this work included the fitting of replenishment at sea equipment, fresh water evaporator, extra radio and naval communication equipment and the conversion of extra diesel and freshwater tanks. A permanent Royal Naval party was embarked to man the communications and generally assist in our dealings with the military. The cargo consisted mainly of equipment for 2 Para and 656 Squadron AAC … vehicles … 3 Scout helicopters and associated stores … a large quantity of reserve ammunition and general military equipment. Personnel were embarked from these units, with a detachment from the RAMC.

On passage to Portland Naval Base we carried out RAS trials and whilst at the base various calibrations and other trials were completed. We sailed from Portland on Sunday 25th for a rendezvous with the ATLANTIC CONVEYOR off Plymouth that evening. We then sailed in company to Freetown. During this passage the embarked force spent much of their time in training, ranging from PT to small arms firing. The scouts of 656 Squadron were involved in both practice flying and the movement of stores between the two ships. For our part we had to learn how to handle the ship to obtain the best conditions for decklandings, we also had to give serious thought on how to prepare the ship for war. Two days were spent in Freetown (2nd - 4th May) before leaving in company with the NORLAND, the ATLANTIC CONVEYOR having sailed the day earlier. We were all thankful to leave Freetown due to the oppressive heat. Now topped up again with fuel and fresh water we headed to Ascension; during the passage we held Court to King Neptune on 'crossing the line', arriving at Ascension on the 7th. That day was spent making final preparations for our journey south.

On sailing that night we were now part of a much larger group, which included HMS FEARLESS flying the broad pennant of Commodore Clapp, Commodore Amphibious Warfare. The whole atmosphere had now undergone drastic change, ships were darkened, navigation lights extinguished, radar was not to be used and ships were ordered to keep their assigned station. Fortunately the first few nights under these conditions were moonlit! When 'Defence Watches' were instituted, the ships company were divided into two watches so that half the crew were up and alert at any time. Personnel remained in their clothing at all times. Glass fittings were taped up to prevent shattering and furniture was securely lashed down. Extra lookouts were posted and the engine room manning increased. During the passage south more ships joined the group, notable additions were the CANBERRA and several of the larger Royal Fleet Auxiliaries. We were now escorted by an increasing number of frigates and destroyers. Opportunity was taken to RAS both fuel and food. Apart from one particularly bad thirty-six hour period, the weather was better than had been expected. By the 18th May we had joined with the Main Naval Task Force in the Total Exclusion Zone and soon we were experiencing our first 'Action Stations' as naval escorts picked electronic emissions indicating the possible threat of enemy aircraft and sonar contacts warned of a possible presence of submarines. We had for our own defence at this time an armament of machine guns and 'Blowpipe missiles'.

On the 20th May we changed to a much tighter formation now we were to become part of the main amphibious landing force and the consequence of this was to detach from the main task force. Our group now consisted of five RFA logistic landing ships (LSLs), two RFA supply ships, a strong frigate escort and three merchant ships, namely CANBERRA, NORLAND and ourselves. The principal units of this amphibious force were the assault ships FEARLESS and INTREPID. The weather during this phase of the operation had deteriorated, but it gave us the cover which we required.

It was well reported on how the Amphibious force navigated through Falkland South that night and into San Carlos Water, successfully disembarking our troops and equipment before the enemy had realised the extent of our operation. For myself, entering San Carlos just before dawn on what promised to be a sunny winter's day and seeing the CANBERRA lying at anchor typified a scene from a cruise brochure, only to have it broken by the harsh reality of war as tracer flew through the pale light of dawn over Fanning Head.

As we anchored in our allocated position, the sky was alive with helicopters ferrying men and equipment ashore. Our first load to go was the Battery of six 105 mm field guns with their ready-to-use ammunition. The sky was cloudless and would afford no cover from air attack. The first indication of impending action was an overall quietness and calm in the anchorage as most helicopters found cover on shore. HMS INTREPID, in the next anchorage to ours, broke the silence by sounding her whistle in a pre-conceived plan to alert our forces ashore. In this first attack by Mirage, Skyhawks and Pucara on the beachhead, the action was concentrated around the CANBERRA and NORLAND and during this engagement INTREPID brought down a Pucara with her seacat missile. In subsequent attacks the length of San Carlos Water was overflown, now the LSLs and ourselves were becoming targets. There were some near misses especially one bomb that dropped between us and INTREPID. On these occasions our ship brought its 'main armament' of machine guns to bear and whilst I claim no hits we did fire in anger which was a great boost for morale. Throughout the day we continued as an operating deck for helicopters, whilst simultaneously discharging equipment into landing craft from the stern door. As we waited for the setting sun to bring an end to the air attacks on the beachhead, all on board had now realised the meaning of the 'Longest Day'. All credit must be given to the action of the warships that had been deployed in defence of the landing forces. We sailed early Saturday morning from the beachhead to rendezvous with the main task force, in company with CANBERRA and NORLAND.

We took this opportunity whilst with the Task Force to alter the ship's paint work. Forces ashore at San Carlos had remarked on how distinctive a target our contrasting colours made us. Therefore we painted the funnel grey and broke up the vessels outline with grey paint where possible. This will I hope explain our rather hideous appearance at present. However if we were successful in putting only one Argentine pilot off making us his target, then it has served its purpose well.

On the 25th May we were ordered to close with the CANBERRA to embark her Sea King flight for passage with us that night to San Carlos. It was during this transfer that we heard in a news broadcast of the Argentine claim that she had been sunk. After this transfer we were to rendezvous with the ATLANTIC CONVEYOR, but that evening before the rendezvous was made, the Task Force came under air attack and she was hit by an Exocet Missile. This loss was felt very deeply on board as we had come a long way together, furthermore our position in the group prior to our meeting with the CANBERRA had been next to hers.

That night we sailed to San Carlos alone. The following day was spent discharging equipment and ammunition, it was relatively peaceful, although there were a number of air raid warnings only one high level bombing run materialised and I think this was directed at land positions several miles away. Before sailing that evening we embarked personnel from 18 Squadron RAF who had lost all but one of their Chinook helicopters on board the ATLANTIC CONVEYOR.

EUROPIC FERRY subsequently returned to the Task Force and two days later proceeded to the logistics waiting area which had been established to the east of the Total Exclusion Zone and further away from the threat of air attacks. Here we remained until the 9th June, our remaining cargo no longer required on shore, two weeks of sailing slowly up and down a designated sector. The highlight of this time was the almost daily rendezvous with the other ships in the area for a transfer of stores and mail. After being a part of the initial landings it was all now something of an anti-climax.

Relief was to occur when we were ordered to proceed with HMS BRILLIANT to meet up with ST. EDMUND and CONTENDER BEZANT; on board the latter were Chinook helicopters for the pilots of 18 Squadron (still embarked onboard). The Chinooks were urgently required ashore presumably to move men and heavy equipment in preparation for the attack on Port Stanley. The plan after blading up one aircraft on CONTENDER BEZANT was to use our deck to hold the aircraft whilst another was prepared on board CONTENDER BEZANT, the pair then flying off in company, repeating this operation until all Chinooks had departed. The weather interfered at this point and delayed the initial transfer which resulted in the first aircraft departing on its own. With the second Chinook on deck we were now subjected to about 36 hours of continuous force 10 and 11 gales, with a heavy swell up to 50 feet at times. Such was the severity of the storm that on several occasions we were in danger of losing the Chinook over the side. On the morning of the 16th the weather had moderated sufficiently and we were able to fly it off.

This was the time that we also received orders to proceed to Port Stanley, and this we did after transferring the remainder of 18 Squadron personnel to the ST.EDMUND. We anchored in Port William (off Stanley) on the morning of the 17th, subsequently moving to the inner harbour to transfer the SatCom team, who were required to establish a communication port at Government House. Since then the ship has moved around the harbour subject to the requirements of the naval authorities, until finally on the 23rd we started loading personnel and equipment for return to the UK, thus bringing to a close what has been probably the most eventful period in this ship's history.

This account is of the small part played by EUROPIC FERRY in the overall operation to restore British sovereignty to the Falkland Islands. I have deliberately omitted the names of any crew members, all of whom conducted themselves with great fortitude during this arduous and at times worrying voyage.

I was privileged to attend a memorial and thanksgiving service in the Church at Port Stanley on Sunday 20th and having listened to the people and heard their story it would have been difficult to understand if we had not sent a force to liberate these people.

The BALTIC FERRY

Captain B C Harrison, (1954-56), has written his account.

I was appointed Master of BALTIC FERRY in early 1982. I was on leave when the vessel was requisitioned about 30th April, with her sister ship NORDIC FERRY. Another of the company's vessels, EUROPIC FERRY had been taken up ten days before, and it seemed only a matter of time before the eyes of the MOD should fall on us, bearing in mind the capability of the vessels for working landing craft and helicopters.

I was asked if I would take the ship to the South Atlantic, and surmising that we would probably get no nearer than South Georgia, I agreed readily enough. Whilst my opposite number took the ship from Felixstowe to Portsmouth and Southampton for outfitting and loading, I went home to wonder what we were going to let ourselves in for.

I joined the vessel in Southampton on 7th May … Replenishment at Sea gear, Satellite communications, helo pads, F.W. generator and extra life-rafts were being fitted. Upper deck bulwarks were cut away and side netting fitted. Loading of ammunition and stores proceeded apace.

We sailed on 9th May, in company with our sister ship, carrying elements of 5th Infantry Brigade, most of their equipment being carried on the two ships. The bulk of the troops were to follow in QE II. Cargo consisted of kerosene, petrol, diesel fuel, airgas, ammunition of all kinds including 105 mm, Blowpipe, Milan, and SS Missiles and phosphorous. We also carried a 105 mm Battery of 4th Field Regiment, 3 Scout helicopters of 656 Squadron

Army Air Corps, vehicles, including Snowcats, belonging to Welsh and Scots Guards, REME workshops, 9th Field Ambulance and the Gurkha Regiment. Small detachments of troops from each unit accompanied their kit. With a Royal Navy party of fourteen to handle helicopter work and communications, the number of service personnel on board totalled about 130.

The civilian crew of forty included a completely volunteer complement of Townsend Officers, amongst them Bill Langton, Second Officer, (1967-69), I also had Lieutenant-Commander, Ian Webb, RN, to keep an eye on me, and translate the gobbeldy-gook from Northwood. It was his job to work us up to a warlike pitch on the way South.

We did a quick practice RAS with a German Fleet Tanker off Portland … all ours were busy further south by then! A few last minute stores came out by helicopter, for our first deck landings, … we completed nearly 1000 in the next four months … then set off for Ascension in company with NORDIC.

After a quick stop at Freetown to top with fuel, we were told to stand off 20' from Ascension for a day, and helicopters brought out more stores for the Task Force and twenty RAF Harrier technicians.

We left Ascension on 20th May, and the initial landings by British Troops were made soon after. Needless to say we listened closely to all BBC World Service bulletins from then on.

We began blackout and defence station drills, and the troops did small arms and artillery practice, and we flew our helicopters for practice landings. As we were in close company and keeping radio silence, one's morse and Aldis lamp skills, long atrophied after fourteen years in ferries, came back quickly!

A few days later QE II overtook us. We had been expecting to meet her and spent 48 hours shifting and sorting cargo, looking for items they required, but in the event time and weather did not permit and the operation was cancelled. All this time we had been heading for South Georgia, but about 27th May we were split up and given separate routes towards the Falklands. QE II meanwhile transferred her troops to NORLAND, CANBERRA and the RFA ships.

BALTIC arrived in the LOLA (Logistics Loitering Area) on 29th May. On 31st May, we rendezvoused with the Carrier Battle Group, and spent a wild afternoon transferring the stores we had to the various RFAs by helicopter, until the deteriorating weather and darkness called a halt. It was now our turn to land the second wave of troops and as night fell we formed up with NORLAND, BLUE ROVER and ATLANTIC CAUSEWAY with HMS BRILLIANT as escort. We headed round the North of East Falkland. Off Cape Dolphin we changed escorts and HMS YARMOUTH and HMS MINERVA shepherded us into San Carlos water in total darkness. Unloading commenced immediately by LCV and Mexefloat. At first light our army helicopters flew off and Sea Kings and Wessex got busy unloading us and the other vessels in the bay. Most of our mobile equipment was off in the first few hours. We had several air raid warnings Red, but saw no aircraft.

On 2nd June we re-fuelled from RFA TIDEPOOL, and left San Carlos that night for the holding area. Anchorage space was tight and other ships with other equipment went in to take our place.

The 3rd June found us out with the Task Force working helicopters all day in patches of dense fog with RFAs, before proceeding to the waiting area now renamed 'Tug and Repair and Logistic's area' (TRALA). This was, we were assured, outside Argentine Air Force range, but the discovery of two aircraft drop tanks floating in our patch gave us something to think about.

We stooged about until 7th June when HMS ANDROMEDA took us to Cape Dolphin, thence HMS PLYMOUTH took us to Fanning Head. We re-entered San Carlos and re-anchored before dawn. About noon the first of the day's air raid warnings found us very impressed. High-flying enemy aircraft were reported approaching the sound, but after HMS EXETER brought one down with a Sea Dart we saw no more of them.

Unloading of ammunition and fuel continued. Next day an attack by Seahawks resulted in HMS PLYMOUTH, guarding the head of the sound, being hit, but bringing down two of her attackers. We watched anxiously as she anchored half a mile away and brought the fires under control. Later, Harriers were based on Port San Carlos and their mere presence in the air was enough to deter further attacks.

On the night of the eighth, helicopters kept flying in and out of Ajax Bay long after dark, and we gathered that many casualties were coming in from Bluff Cove.

On the 10th we left San Carlos for the TRALA, and this time we carried twelve Special Category Argentine prisoners for 'outward transfer'. Whilst the troops fought for Tumbledown and Mt Longdon and Mt Kent, we watched the gunfire from our position in the TRALA.

On the 13th we spent the whole day with the Carrier

Battle Group and RFAs receiving by helicopter all the medical supplies they could spare for Ajax Bay.

We worked helos with REGENT, OLMEDA, BLUE ROVER, BAYLEAF, HERMES, INVINCIBLE and CANBERRA.

On the night of 14th June, we re-entered San Carlos having had a bit of a scare on the run in when just before changing escorts with the outward convoy, which included our colleagues on the NORDIC FERRY, the outward convoy appeared to be under attack. At any rate a lot of fireworks filled the sky ahead of us; however in the darkness it was hard to see what was what.

We arrived in San Carlos safely and discharged our medical stores. That night we were allocated a temporary anchorage at the entrance to the bay and warned about sabotage. Naturally Murphy's Law came into play *(if something bad can happen it probably will)* and the engine room staff rang the bridge in the small hours and reported 'noises on the hull'. The weather was very bad and divers from FEARLESS could not inspect us for mines for about 36 hours. Naturally we slept with our boots on meanwhile!

On the 15th the foul weather no doubt helped the Argentines to make up their minds and surrender. We stopped unloading, and after 24 hours commenced re-loading some of the huge amounts of equipment and vehicles on the beaches.

On the 25th June we were ordered to Port Stanley, where the ship was anchored and where she remains, acting as a floating warehouse and workshop until suitable buildings and storage are erected ashore. The NORDIC returned home in late July.

The crew of the BALTIC were relieved at the end of August and returned by MV NORLAND to Ascension, and by RAF VC10 to UK.

A third crew relieved the second in November. At the end of January I returned to BALTIC with a fourth crew, including Bill Langton once more, and the vessel should be released from Port Stanley, and we shall have the pleasure of bringing her back to Felixstowe.

THE ROYAL FLEET AUXILIARIES

MEGA RAS ... RFA FORT AUSTIN AND RFA FORT GRANGE

Captain D G M Averill, CBE, (1941-43), remembers.

I am enclosing an extract which will give you a rundown on FORT GRANGE's activities. It does not mention the appalling weather which was an important factor.

Unfortunately with so much night work, my own vision deteriorated and I have been invalided from further sea service. As part of your record I would like there to be a mention of the great backup work carried out by Captain C G Butterworth, RFA, as the Chief Marine Superintendent of the RFA Service. You will be interested to know that FORT GRANGE is now commanded by another OC, Captain B H Rutterford, (1946-48).

The Royal Fleet Auxiliaries, the civilian afloat support arm of the Fleet, are world leaders in the skill called 'RAS' ... Replenishment at Sea. In all weathers these merchant ships (with their embarked stores party of civil servants) manoeuvre to within 200 ft of a Naval ship and both maintain the same course and speed whilst transferring fuel, goods, ammunition and other solid stores. Wherever the Royal Navy ships go, there goes the RFA too … they were in the thick of the action in San Carlos water and elsewhere. Sadly too, they shared the tragedy in the attack on RFAs, SIR GALAHAD and SIR TRISTAM at Bluff Cove.

Like all ships in the operation, FORT AUSTIN performed near miracles of effort and endurance, but for her it started well before the Naval action. In mid-April whilst topping up the ships of the Task Force, she stored a series of ships in a continuous operation for over 26 hours. As one RN ship broke off, another took her place alongside. The operation has since come to be known as the 'megaras' … a record breaking gigantic replenishment at sea.

Her sister ship RFA FORT GRANGE, Capt D G M Averill, CBE, sailed from the United Kingdom on Friday, 14th May 1982, after completing refit one month early and loading maximum cargo in record time. C Flight of 824 Squadron embarked with three Sea Kings, and the journey south was spent training the new ship's company in basic drills and emergency exercises.

On the long journey south, FORT GRANGE was over-flown by an Argentine Hercules. Fortunately it did not drop any bombs, but later bombed the BRITISH WYE in the same area.

The ship arrived in the Total Exclusion Zone on 3rd June to rendezvous with the Carrier Group … in thick fog. Being the first auxiliary stores ship to arrive in the TEZ since the Task Force sailed, she was bulging at the seams with stores and 'goodies'. Many of the Carrier Group ships were so short of food, they were about to break open the emergency 'compo' rations. FORT GRANGE spent eight hectic days replenishing them, using both helicopters and alongside replenishment methods. In addition, two aircraft were on anti-submarine patrol. During this period 25 ships were resupplied with vital stores.

After transferring hundreds of tons of stores, she sailed into Bomb Alley to resupply the beach head and the ships of Bomb Alley.

The next few weeks alternated between rasing and vertreps (stores transfer by helicopter) with the Battle Group, visits to San Carlos water to top up RFAs going home, and embark new stores brought from the UK. GEESPORT, LYCAON, AVELONA STAR and SAXONIA were regular 'customers'. Incidentally, Old Conways were Masters of the first three ships!

LYCAON typifies the information we have. She sailed from Southampton on 4th May, called at South Georgia then to San Carlos water and Port William. Captain H R Lawton, (1951-52), flew home with his crew on 3rd September, as though it all might have been a conventional voyage.

During the spells in San Carlos water, FORT GRANGE supplied stores to Army and Navy Helicopter detachments, and the PoW camps. On one occasion she steamed round to Bluff Cove to Vertrep tons of victuals to RFA SIR GERAINT who was supporting a number of soldiers and trying to get the bomb damaged RFA SIR TRISTAM serviceable again.

On 11th July 1982 while vertrepping stores from HMS LEEDS CASTLE, one of the Sea Kings ditched. The crew were picked up by the HMS LEEDS CASTLE's 'Sea Rider', but the helicopter sank in the heavy swell.

In all, the ship was involved in five air raids but was not actually attacked in any of them. RFA FORT GRANGE spent 107 days in the Total Exclusion Zone during which time she carried out the following:-

208 transfers with 42 HM Ships

65 transfers with 18 Royal Fleet Auxiliary vessels

75 transfers with 29 Merchant vessels

2 transfers with 1 Royal Marine Auxiliary Service ship

29 transfers with 7 shore stations, 10 major consolidations with 7 ships.

She issued the fleet with about 700,000 lbs of potatoes and half a million eggs … some ships have been virtually living on egg 'n chips.

Also issued were 10,500 gallons of draught beer and 21,000 cases of canned beer (at 24 cans per case).

The Flight flew 334 day sorties and 63 night sorties, a total of 867 hours day flying and 154 hours night flying. All this entailed 933 day deck landings and 165 night landings. In addition to this, each time the ship went into either Port San Carlos or Stanley she became the local Spar ship and Heron garage with customers arriving from all directions for food, petrol, a shower and drinks/lunch.

Captain G R Green (1949-51) gives us his recollections.

I was Master of SIR TRISTAM at Fitzroy Creek … or, as the press has it, Bluff Cove … where she was bombed and set on fire, along with her sister ship SIR GALAHAD. It was a whole new experience, and I have the need to replace my Conway tie, plus of course everything else!

He says no more.

The SIR TRISTAM and SIR GALAHAD incidents were bad and some of the casualties at least could have been avoided, if Major Southby-Tailyour had had his way.

Fitzroy Creek is on the east side of East Falkland. It was decided to rush some supporting troops round to take advantage of the military situation, and the two RFAs took on the Welsh Guards and stores. SIR TRISTAM arrived first and commenced to unload supplies … she had relatively few soldiers.

The beach at Fitzroy was not ideal for landing stores and it all took longer than normal. Also Fitzroy was not where they wanted to go … they wanted to go to Bluff Cove. By sea Bluff Cove was only 6 miles, by land a route march of 20 miles as a vital bridge was down, so the Guardsmen decided to stay aboard SIR GALAHAD at anchor until landing craft were free to take them to Bluff Cove.

Major Southby-Tailyour arrived in a landing craft about lunchtime and immediately appreciated the danger the ships were in and told an Army Officer that the ships should be unloaded at once and get out.

His advice does not appear to have been followed and at about 1400, enemy Sky Hawks appeared and the two ships were bombed. 51 people were killed and 46 injured.

It was a justifiable risk sending the ships to Fitzroy, but it has not been explained why the soldiers, if they had to wait aboard, could not have manned the sides with small arms to shoot at the low flying Sky Hawks. Concentrated machine gunfire does put low flying bombing airmen off their stroke. Perhaps it was because the Guard do not have the same training as the Royal Marines and Paras in amphibious warfare, and they had not of course experienced the ferocity of the enemy attack in the early days at San Carlos.

Captain Green was decorated for his services and the citation reads:

'SIR TRISTAM joined the Amphibious Task Group at Ascension Island and rapidly took up the challenge. From the arrival of the amphibious ships at San Carlos on 21/5/82 to June 1982, SIR TRISTAM was under constant threat of attack. For a period of a week, repeated air attacks were pressed home on the anchorage when the very lightly-armed ship had to protect herself while continuing to off-load important military equipment.

She was the first Landing Ship Logistic to make the run to Fitzroy. The task had to be unescorted and meant lying at anchor by day off Fitzroy in an exposed position without benefit of adequate air defence or warning. It was while there that the ship, still well loaded with ammunition, came under fierce surprise air attack and suffered the damage which caused her to be damaged and on fire. It is greatly to Captain Green's credit that he was successful in getting all his people off the ship with the exception of two crewmen killed by one of the bombs which hit the ship. Captain Green by his personal example and courage throughout the period inspired his crew to do all that was asked of him and them, far beyond the normal call of duty.

THE AFTERMATH

On the 15th June the fighting stopped, the war was won.

The Merchant Navy still have the job of ferrying between Port Stanley and Ascension and some ships have only recently come home.

There were few Merchant Navy casualties, eight killed altogether as far as we calculate … five in SIR GALAHAD, two in SIR TRISTAM and one in ATLANTIC CONVEYOR.

When the surrender was announced on the BBC television, there was a collection of Service Chiefs and politicians to comment. They paid tribute to the fighting Services, the Dock Yard Mateys, those getting the stores together, indeed everyone concerned save one … not one word about the Merchant Navy.

When asked about this later, The Right Honourable David Steel replied: "No discourtesy was meant when I paid tribute to the Armed Forces and omitted to mention the crucial role played by the Merchant Navy. Please rest assured your point is well taken."

The Right Honourable Roy Hattersley said: "Your point is well made. Should I be asked on some future occasion to comment further on the military aspects of the Falklands crisis, I shall bear your remarks in mind".

The Right Honourable Edward du Cann said: "If you do not mind my saying so I think you are being unduly sensitive. Many public tributes have been paid to the Merchant Navy in the House of Commons and elsewhere and very properly too."

It is not that they intended to omit the Merchant Navy. At the moment of victory it obviously never occurred to them that the Merchant Navy had anything to do with it or they would have included them in the praise. The Merchant

Navy tends to be forgotten by the public as a whole save for the prestige ships.

The Royal Navy does not forget the Merchant Navy. At the end of the campaign the two services were working as one. The RN also did their best to see the ships of the MN received a good welcome home too, and every Officer of either service who was there has the highest respect for the skill and work of the other's service.

THE DECORATIONS awarded to Conways:

Clarke C	Master,	EUROPIC FERRY	OBE
Green G	Master,	RFA SIR TRISTAM	DSC
Redmond S	Master,	RFA TIDESPRING	OBE

Mr R B Lough received a Commendation from Admiral Fieldhouse. H was the Chief Officer of M V NORLAND, a North Sea ferry taken up from trade for the Falklands Operation. Throughout the deployment of the ship with the Task Force he gave tireless active support and thoughtful cooperation to the military embarked personnel. He was instrumental in devising the method finally used for troop disembarkation during the initial landing phase. When the ship came under attack his courage and resolve were everywhere evident as he moved between decks … an example to the ship's Officers and Men.

NORLAND's only boats are GRP lifeboats, designed to be launched from davits, but requiring considerable skill for recovery. During the night of 10th June 1982 on passage he lowered and took away a lifeboat to effect a successful rescue of a man overboard.

He was commended for his willingness, initiative and fortitude in ensuring the successful achievement of MV NORLAND's task.

Chief Officer R B Lough writes:

'At the end of August, Captain Ellerby returned home with half of the crew from Ascension Island and I took over command of NORLAND. I returned home at the end of September with the remainder of the original crew for a spell of well-earned leave.

'I returned to Ascension at the end of October for a further spell in command of NORLAND and had the pleasant task of returning Lady Hunt to the Islands. It was while we were in Port Stanley in November that we had some engine trouble and had to miss one trip up to Ascension to enable repairs to be carried out. The highlight of our stay in Stanley was an invitation to dinner at Government House with Sir Rex and Lady Hunt. It was a memorable night which ended at two in the morning, driving a Gemini inflatable across Stanley Harbour in a Force Eight gale back to the ship. Fortunately there are no breathalysers in the Falkland Islands!

'I flew back to the Falklands in December courtesy of the RAF, in the back of a Hercules! Quite an experience! Twelve hours sitting on a pile of luggage, and to think it's the most expensive flight in the world!!

'NORLAND arrived back at Hull on May 1st for a refit and went back into service across the North Sea on April 19th … one year and two days after being requisitioned.

'I am now back on NORLAND as Chief Officer with occasional spells as Master. I must say it is nice to be back on the run after the events of last year. NORLAND was very lucky to have survived the campaign as the Argentine Air Force was very good and gave us quite a hard time last May. However, we were lucky and survived and I must say that looking back it was 95% hard work, 5% sheer terror, but I wouldn't have missed it for the world.'

CONCLUSION

Sydney Miller

My wife and I stayed put here in Port Stanley and so suffered the full two and half months of invasion. The Argy so-called-army here was about the most undisciplined rabble I have ever seen. Many Stanley residents locked their houses and took refuge on sheep stations. We were glad we stayed put here during the occupation as the houses evacuated by residents nearly all had their homes broken into and heavily looted and disgustingly soiled.

However, that is now gone with good thanks to Margaret Thatcher, the British people behind her and those magnificent fighting troops who got a tremendous reception when they reached us.

We now have a garrison of some 3000 troops, RAF and Navy and many ships in the inner and outer harbours. We are a bit jammed, but glad to have them all. They have done, and are doing, a first class job of clearing up the filthy mess and damage caused by the Argentine troops.

Stanley is slowly trying to get back to something like normal, but with many troops which of course includes their very heavy vehicles, for the like of which Stanley roads are not good enough. The town is in a bit of a mess with badly pot-holed roads. We get on extremely well with all the troops and the billeting has now eased up with the army villages of Portacabins going up and the moving out to the main sheep farming areas. Here the high command has installed training areas, especially on the large stations, which have allowed full use of their hill areas for artillery training and Harrier bombing practice. These areas are very large … thousands of acres with rocky hills up to 2,000 feet. As the General told me, nowhere in Britain could they get such unrestricted land use and with the Argentine refusal to consider hostilities at an end, the Navy and the RAF are on continual alert and do their patrolling of the 150 mile zone all the time, which in itself is continual training for those services.

The Islands will of course never be the same, but it must alter anyway as we need investment and development and most important we need people. The population is too small. There is a dearth of labour of all sorts, both heavy work and office work. Sheep stations are short-handed too, but to a fair extent automation has eased that burden … they are fully mechanised and most of the large places have well-equipped machine shops. We know many people seem to want to emigrate here, but we have got to build many more houses yet. Stanley is handicapped to an extent by the many mine fields, mostly unmapped, left behind by the Argies. No beach near the town is safe for any child or adult and is likely to stay that way. Mine fields on ground areas are gradually getting cleared by the Royal Engineers, but it is a slow job with no maps left by the enemy. Booby traps are still being found by the Royal Engineers, and even these have been found in the town and can only have been designed to kill or maim civilians. Argentina is a Nazi-minded nation as far as its military Government is concerned and they had their Gestapo installed here during the short war.

However, everybody is cheerful enough and the incoming new citizens, mostly as yet official, are discovering seemingly to their astonishment that these are very lovely, rugged islands, but with a temperate climate throughout the year which never reaches the extremes you get in Britain.

To date we know that the following Old Conways, in addition to those mentioned above, served in the Falklands:

Captain A W Kinghorn, (1949-51) … AVELONA STAR.

Lieutenant-Commander M Manning, RN, (1962-64) … HMS ARROW.

P Hughes (1968-70) … St Helena.

Rear-Admiral J P Edwards, MVO, (1941-44) … Deputy Chief of Fleet Support

Captain J A M Taylor, (1947-49) … BRITISH DART.

Captain H R Lawton, (1951-52) … LYCAON.

CHAPTER THREE

THE CONWAY NOTABLES

Alfred Wright Adcock. (1898-99)

He was born in 1885 in Nottingham and joined CONWAY at 13, and on leaving joined the Merchant Marine. A Second Officer of the INDRABARAH (Tyser Line) he performed two rescues when the vessel went aground on the Rangitikei coast (NZ) in 1913. As a result he was decorated by King George V at Buckingham Palace, and also received rewards from the Royal Humane Society and the Liverpool Shipwreck and Humane Society. During WWI he was First Officer on troop ships. He left the Merchant Navy in 1923 and emigrated to New Zealand, where he took up farming. He gave this up due to ill health, and subsequently worked for the City Council of Palmerston North. He retired in 1955, and died in 1957.

Wing Commander Robert S Allen, DSO, DFC. (Years not known)

Born in Manchester in 1914, Robert Allen was educated at Westfield High School, Manchester and HMS CONWAY and joined the RAF as a pupil pilot in 1935. He was promoted to Squadron Leader in 1939. During June 1940 whilst en-route to bomb a target, he observed a Heinkel III and despite 'bad weather conditions and intense darkness' he manoeuvred his aircraft to enable Sergeant Williams (WOP/AG) to fire at the enemy aircraft and shoot it down. Soon after, the same tactics were employed against a Junker 87 with the same result. Squadron Leader Allen then continued to his objective and bombed the target successfully. He was flying Hampdens with No. 49 Squadron at the time, and was awarded the Distinguished Flying Cross (DFC) for this action. The award of the Bar to his DFC followed in October 1940 while still with No. 49 Squadron. Following promotion to Wing Commander, he then went to No. 106 Squadron at RAF Coningsby. On 24th July 1941, Wing Commander Allen led a daylight attack through heavy anti aircraft fire and fighter opposition against the German battle cruiser GNEISENAU, which was in dry dock at Brest. For his leadership on this operation, he was awarded the Distinguished Service Order (DSO). After leaving No. 106 Squadron, he served on the Air Staff Mission in China between 8th July 1943 and mid-August 1945. On 13th February 1945, he was awarded the Cloud and Banner decoration (Special Rosette), an award confirmed by the President of the Nationalist Government of China. After leaving the RAF, he became a publican. He died in 1982.

W H Baker. (Years not known)
Burning of the VOLTURNO … extracted from the *Liverpool Mercury,* October 18th 1913.

'The awful tragedy in mid-Atlantic by which 136 persons lost their lives through the burning of the emigrant ship VOLTURNO (3602 tons), has startled and horrified the public almost as much as did the awful TITANIC, 18 months ago.

The heavy death-toll is due to the fact that the fire broke out during a raging tempest, so that although the VOLTURNO had more than sufficient boats to carry those on board, they could only launch with a grave risk of being dashed to pieces or swamped when in the water. That so large a proportion of those on board were rescued was due to the fact that she had wireless installation. Her pleas for help were heard widely over the Atlantic, and eleven liners immediately converged on her, but heavy seas effectually prevented rescue work.

VOLTURNO launched seven boats, the first boat swung under the stern and the propeller literally smashed her to matchwood, cutting the unfortunate occupants to pieces. Three more were dashed to pieces as she rolled in the great seas, two reached the water safely but were swamped, killing all onboard. Under such terrible conditions rescue work seemed impossible. Many attempts were made to send rescue boats, but all failed.

VOLTURNO's Master became desperate and called for volunteers to show the other Captains that it was not impossible to launch their boats. One got as far as the GOSSER KURFURST, but the boat was smashed and was almost lost. VOLTURNO's Master sent a final desperate message, "My God! Can't stand this longer. Our boat has gone. Send me some boats!" The Captains of the other boats replied, "We have tried our best. The sea is too heavy and no boat could live in it."

Baker, Second Officer of the Leyland steamer, DEVONIAN, launched a boat and eventually managed to get a lifeboat alongside. He later recalled: "Early in the morning following our arrival on the scene of the disaster, I determined to make an attempt to reach the burning vessel. 'Neck or nothing, let us go' I said to the men. A crew of eight agreed to go out on the boisterous sea, amidst perilous conditions. When we were near to the vessel we could see there would be a rush by those on board to escape. We called to those in charge to keep back the men, who were pressing forward, and to let us save the women and children first. Officers used their fists to drive the men back, and some of them went down like ninepins."

The work was carried out with the most considerable danger. Sparks were flying, the heat on the sides of the vessel was intense, and the smoke was blinding. From time to time some relict of the fire, such as a disjoined derrick or piece of the funnel, would tumble into the water, and might have easily injured rescuers and rescued alike. We could see the smoke coming up between the beams of the deck, and the men were almost standing in flames. During the night the scene was horrible. Shrieking was continuous and several of the women held up their babies and outlined them in the blaze, and begged of us to come and rescue them. Although Baker made several more rescue trips, no other boats dared make the same journey until a tanker appeared and spilled oil onto the raging waters.

He was awarded the Marine Medal of The Liverpool Shipwreck and Humane Society, the Board Of Trade Sea Gallantry Medal and the medal of The Life Saving Benevolent Association of New York. He was also presented with a solid silver tea service by Leyland Line.

Earl of Balfour. (1941-44)

The 4th Earl of Balfour, who died on June 27th aged 77, was once the only Viscount to be an Able Seaman in the Merchant Navy.

In the pre-1999 House of Lords, he was also known as the bane of the parliamentary draftsmen. This was because, being dyslexic, and hence often having to consult a dictionary, he scrutinised each Bill with absolute objectivity, detecting mistakes that skilled proof readers had missed.

On one occasion he raised 53 objections to a government Housing Bill, chiefly on grounds of misspellings and typographical errors, but also citing graver flaws such as transposed sentences. Fifty of his objections were accepted … believed to be a record … and the Bill withdrawn. The government minister who had introduced the Bill remarked that, though he congratulated His Lordship, it was through gritted teeth.

Gerald Arthur James Balfour, the son of the 3rd Earl of Balfour, was born on December 23rd 1925. The Earldom was created in 1922 for the former Tory Prime Minister Arthur Balfour, Gerald's great-uncle. Arthur Balfour had succeeded his own uncle, the 3rd Marquis of Salisbury, in the premiership in 1902 and held it till 1905. The Balfours before that had been lairds for generations of Balbirnie in Fife.

Gerald was educated at Eton and the training school HMS CONWAY. Gerald's father had also hoped to join the Royal Navy but, he too being dyslexic, had misspelled his forename and surname on his entrance paper, and was not admitted.

During the Second World War Gerald served in the Merchant Marine. On his first voyage he was torpedoed by the Japanese, and spent a week in an open boat in the Indian Ocean before being rescued.

On the death of his grandfather four months before the War's end, Balfour inherited the courtesy title of Viscount Traprain. He continued in the Merchant Navy after peace came, serving as deck-hand aboard the four-master 3,200-ton barque PAMIR in a voyage carrying tallow, wool and clothes from well-wishers in New Zealand to Britain's 'Displaced Persons' … as the homeless were then called. At that time he wore a beard and was known to his shipmates as 'Gerry'.

Among his later distinctions, Balfour was President of the Cape Horners, originally an association exclusively of people who had rounded Cape Horn before the mast, that is to say as ordinary crew members of tall ships. Latterly, yachtsmen have been admitted.

In his Merchant Navy days Balfour was a member of the New Zealand Seamen's Union. By the late 1960s, he was more sympathetic to capitalism, and was Chairman of a Scottish bottled water company exporting to places as faraway as South America. In June 1969 he became Chairman of Bruntons, a Musselburgh steel wire manufacturer, but resigned eight months later after a boardroom dispute. He also farmed in East Lothian, where lay the family estate of Whittinghame, near Haddington, and during the 1960s and early 1970s sat as an East Lothian County Councillor.

In later life Balfour turned increasingly to public debate. In the House of Lords he spoke on soil erosion in the Middle East, urging the government to enlist Israeli politicians and Zionist funds to fight it. There was a dual family element in this. His aunt, Lady Evelyn Balfour, had founded the Soil Association. Moreover, that Israel existed at all was largely due to his great-uncle, the 1st Earl, who, as Foreign Secretary in Lloyd George's Coalition Government, had in 1917 issued the Balfour Declaration, announcing support for a Jewish national state.

Gerald Balfour also aired his views in The Telegraph's 'letters page'. These opinions were so wide-ranging as would provoke today the charge 'unfocused'; yet they were largely sensible. In the 1970s he criticised the Wilson government's public housing policy. He argued that the 1965 and 1974 Rent Acts had deliberately reduced the availability of privately rented accommodation, obliging tenants increasingly to take what was offered by local authorities and housing associations, yet with no security of tenure.

He had a knack of anticipating the future. In the early 1980s he was urging that telephones be metered, so that users could judge how big a bill they were running up. In the mid-1980s he called for reform of the rates, arguing that the local authorities' role in providing services should be reduced and central government's increased. A few years later, along with erosion of councils' powers by Whitehall, came the Poll Tax.

In the late 1990s Balfour was on a four-man Parliamentary Commission in Scotland that had to adjudicate in a dispute between Glasgow's Burrell Collection trustees and Glasgow Council's museum director. The latter wanted to be able to exchange items from the Collection with those of other places to boost falling attendance figures.

The trustees feared that breaking the terms of the bequest, which forbade such dispersals, would put off potential future donors. All four Commissioners were hereditary peers, which enraged progressives. That the 4th Earl of Balfour was also a Freemason, and had called the handgun ban after the 1996 Dunblane Massacre a 'news-media-inspired panic', damned him further in liberal circles.

Balfour was, in fact, far from a diehard Conservative. The Bill he caused to be withdrawn was one put forward by the John Major administration. Nor was he opposed to the people's will. In one of the last debates in the old House of Lords before most hereditaries were ejected, he stated that it was not for their lordships to oppose Scottish devolution since it had been voted for. Yet he was certain that the Bill needed amendments and improvements.

Vice Admiral Sir David Brown, KCB. (1941-45)

A gifted and incisive RN staff officer who twice played a crucial background role in making the 1982 victory in the Falklands war possible.

Deep defence cuts made by the Secretary of State, Denis Healey, during Harold Wilson's Labour administrations of the late 1960s, had effectively confined the Royal Navy to the North Atlantic and the Mediterranean. Under Edward Heath's Conservative government of the early 1970s, Brown, as Director of Naval Operations and Trade, successfully argued the case for annual naval forays to such areas as the Far East and the South Atlantic. This revival of the old custom of 'showing the flag' would remind the world of Britain's abiding foreign interests, such as the Falkland Islands. It also meant that recruits could once again be attracted by the slogan, 'Join the navy and see the world'. The future Admiral of the Fleet, Lord Lewin, who was Chief of the Defence Staff at the time of the Falklands war, was then Vice Chief of Naval Staff, and pushed Brown's idea through the Ministry of Defence. A series of deployments a long way east (and south) ensued.

Ironically it was under Margaret Thatcher's first administration that another massive defence cut, including slashing the fleet and removing the last vestige of an already minimal presence in the South Atlantic, led the Argentine military junta to think that the Falklands were theirs for the taking. Thatcher's Defence Secretary, John Nott, who had proposed severely reducing the fleet, including the sale of the two aircraft carriers then in service, believed that nothing could be done once the Argentine army had taken the inhospitable archipelago 8,000 miles from Britain. Thatcher was furious but frustrated. There was much wringing of hands until Admiral Sir Henry Leach, the Chief of Naval Staff, marched into parliament in his full uniform to seek out the ministerial conclave. Lewin was on an official visit to New Zealand and Leach was acting as his deputy. He persuaded Thatcher that the navy could dispatch a task force 'by the weekend' to take back the Falklands. Three nuclear attack submarines set off at once, while the bulk of the surface fleet was sent to the South Atlantic along with some 3,000 Royal Marines and paratroopers in commandeered liners. By this time, Rear Admiral Brown was in the key post of Assistant Chief of Defence Staff (Operations), and it fell to him, alongside Lewin, to brief the daily meetings of the War Cabinet in London on events in the South Atlantic. His briefings impressed Thatcher and all who heard them.

The son of a naval Officer, Brown was born in London on 28th November 1927, and joined CONWAY. He was at or near the top of his intake in several subjects, won prizes and was a Cadet Captain. Poor eyesight meant that it took him five attempts to get into the navy. His determination won him a place in the last week of the Second World War at the age of 17. He became a specialist in anti-submarine warfare and commanded eight vessels, from a gunboat, via minesweepers, to frigates and a frigate squadron, and finally took charge of one of the latest guided missile destroyers.

His inability to suffer fools gladly extended to the top of the service, and probably explained why such a gifted Officer never made full Admiral. He ran a tight ship, drove his juniors hard, dismissing several, but did not suck up to his superiors, as tough taskmasters sometimes do. He was once called aboard HMS VANGUARD, Britain's last battleship and the flagship of Admiral Sir Philip Vian, the Commander-in-Chief Home Fleet. Vian was furious because Brown's ship had failed to dip its colours in salute to him as it entered harbour. After being bawled out at considerable volume, Brown was cool enough to tell Vian that, as a ship's Captain, he was entitled to be piped aboard the flagship ... and had therefore not been properly saluted either.

Brown saw active service as an Operations Officer in the confrontation with Indonesia in the 1960s, and held several staff posts, including with Nato. His last position was as Flag Officer, Plymouth, before he retired in 1985 with a KCB. He became a company director and, for a time, was chairman of the governors at Broadmoor hospital. Always a keen fisherman, he gave a lot of time to angling organisations, as well as to Trinity House.

Captain W H Coombes. (1907-09)

From the end of the war through to the General Strike in 1926 many deep-seated grievances in the Merchant Navy surfaced. Merchant Navy officers felt undervalued, underpaid and underrepresented. They formed their first union, the British Merchant Service League in 1919, but this failed in 1921. Captain Coombes left the sea in 1921 determined to improve their status and circumstances. He formed the Navigators and General Insurance Company to enable Officers to insure themselves against the loss of their professional certificates following an official enquiry into the loss of a ship, a collision or other accident.

In 1925 he wrote and paid for the publication of a book, 'The Nation's Keymen' in which he argued the case for the professional status and role of the Merchant Navy Officer.

His work inspired others and in 1928 he was influential in the formation of the Officers' (MN) Federation through which many British and Commonwealth Officers' Associations worked together on key issues. In 1932 he formed 'The Watch Ashore' to represent Officers' wives. Determined to make the Government improve the lot of Officers, he organised a 23,000 signature petition that resulted in the creation of the Merchant Navy Officers' Pension Fund and the Central Board for the Training of Officers for the Merchant Navy. In 1935 he formed the Navigators & Engineers Officers Union.

Vice-Admiral Sir David Clutterbuck, KBE, CB.
(1926-29)

He took part in many famous wartime actions in the Mediterranean and the Far East. He commanded the newly commissioned BLAKE which was the last conventional cruiser to be built for the Royal Navy. Promoted to Rear-Admiral in 1963, he was Chief of Staff to the C-in-C Home Fleet. His final tour as Vice-Admiral was as Deputy Supreme Allied Commander Atlantic, 1966-68. He died on December 13th, 2008, aged 95.

Rear-Admiral Douglas Everett, CB, CBE, MBE, DSO.
(1911-13)

Executive Officer in AJAX from 1937 and fought

in the Battle of the River Plate. As Chief Staff Officer to Force V, he planned the invasion of Sicily, 1942-43. In command of Aircraft Carrier ARBITER in Far East, 1944 45. Commanded DUKE OF YORK, 1947-49. Flag Officer, Ground Training, 1949-51. President of the Admiralty Interview Board, 1951-52, when he retired.

Francis Murray Russell Flint. (1933-35)

Marine artist son of the well known artist of the same name. He painted the Second World War Honours Board which now hangs in the CONWAY Chapel at Birkenhead Priory.

Venerable Simon Golding. (1961-63)

Archdeacon for the Royal Navy and Honorary Chaplain to Her Majesty the Queen since March, 1997. He was made Honorary Canon of Gibraltar Cathedral in 1998. He was appointed Chaplain of the Fleet and Director General of the Naval Chaplaincy Service on June 1st 2000.

Born in Chelmsford in 1946, his childhood was spent in India and he was educated in India and in the United Kingdom. He attended St. Xavier's School, Jaipur, the Junior School, Feldsted, the Bishop's School, Poona and HMS CONWAY before starting his career at sea.

Captain George Hunt, DSO, DSC, RAN. (1920-22)

George Hunt was born in Scotland in 1916. At the age of 14 he commenced Royal Navy Reserve training at

HMS CONWAY. During the 1930s he served variously with the Royal Navy in cruisers and merchant shipping companies such as Blue Funnel Line as a Junior Officer. 1937 saw him serving in a cruiser with the RN. As part of the preparation for war in 1938, he was selected along with one hundred others to serve full time with the RN. In 1939 he was a survivor from the submarine UNITY when she was rammed and sunk in the North Sea. In 1940 he was appointed second in command of HM Submarine PROTEUS. During the period 1940/41, PROTEUS sank twelve ships and eventually the submarine 'retired hurt' after a collision with an Italian Cruiser.

In 1942 he qualified for Command and later that year took Command of HMS ULTOR until the end of 1944. During that period Captain Hunt sank twenty-eight ships, was awarded 2 DSOs, 2 DSCs and was Mentioned in Despatches twice.

George Hunt rose to the rank of Commodore and eventually retired in 1960 when he joined the RAN Emergency list at the rank of Captain. During his final years in the RN, he served as 'Teacher' in the Submarine Service. This meant he had the responsibility for training and qualifying submarine Commanding Officers.

Other appointments included Command of a destroyer and the 7th Frigate Squadron, an appointment in the NATO Area, Chief of Staff to Flag Officer Submarines and finally Senior Naval Officer West Indies as a Commodore (One star).

He settled in Queensland in 1963 joining the RANEM as a Captain. Since going to Queensland he served with the Company of Master Mariners, and has been President of the United Services Institute. George was elected Patron of the Submarine Association of Queensland in 1990.

John Masefield, OM, D Litt. (1891-94)

John was born in Ledbury, Herefordshire, where the family solicitor's business continues to this day. He was orphaned young and brought up by an aunt. It was aboard the CONWAY that Masefield's love for story telling grew. While in the ship, he listened to the stories told about sea lore. He continued to read, and felt that he was to become a writer and storyteller himself. After CONWAY he went to sea, but to his great regret had to come ashore … he suffered extreme seasickness. His poem 'Roadways' explains his calling for the sea.

After many years in New York he returned to the UK. He served as a medical orderly in the Great War even though old enough to be exempt from military service. He became Poet Laureate in May 1930 and was judged to be everyone's poet and a poet's poet.

He wrote many poems about the sea and a considerable number of verses especially for the CONWAY, including The Gulls, for the masting of the new figurehead in 1938 and to commemorate the centenary in 1959. He wrote of his CONWAY years in his book 'New Chum' published in the UK and USA and was her official historian producing two editions of The Conway in 1933 and 1953. He was President of the Conway Club 1930-34. He is interred in Poets' Corner in Westminster Abbey.

Frank Henry Mason, RBA, Rl. (1880-82)

He was born at Seaton Carew, County Durham in October 1866. It was during his time at sea after CONWAY that he discovered his interest in painting and in order to devote more time to this subject, he returned to shore and studied under Albert Strange at the Scarborough School of Art.

He became an official war artist during the First World War whilst serving as a Lieutenant in the Royal Naval Volunteer Reserves. Between the wars he painted many commissions for shipping companies, especially Everards. He also designed many posters for the LNER, Great Western and NER railways. During the Second World War he worked for the Directorate of Camouflage, Naval Division. He was a prolific marine painter and his love of the sea is reflected in both his oils and watercolours. He specialised in subjects as diverse as commercial and naval vessels throughout the world to yachting regattas. He continued to live in Scarborough and painted until his death in 1965.

James Moody (1904-06)

Sixth Officer of the TITANIC, Moody was on the Bridge at the time of the sinking. He received the fateful message from the lookouts that there was an iceberg ahead … he had earlier told them to be on special lookout for them. He initiated the first avoiding action. Fifth Officer Harold Godfrey Lowe had an encounter with Moody while they filled boats 14 and 16. Lowe remarked that he had seen five boats lowered, and one of the next two ought to have an Officer. Moody answered, "You go. I will get in another boat". Lowe survived, Moody did not. After overseeing the safe loading of a number of lifeboats, he was last seen alone on deck. There is a special TITANIC exhibition in the Merseyside Maritime Museum, including the CONWAY's Moody Cup.

Moody's last actions were recalled by Geoffrey Marcus in 'The Maiden Voyage'.

'Chief Officer Wilde's efforts to avert panic, maintain order and discipline, and get the last of the boats loaded and lowered to the water, were valiantly supported by the youngest of the Officers, James Moody. Long before this, the latter should by rights have gone away in one of the boats along with the other Junior Officers, but the seamen left on board were all too few as it was for the work that had to be done. Moody therefore stayed with the ship to the end and was the means of saving many a life that would otherwise have been lost.'

There is a rose marble memorial plaque bearing James's name in the Church of St. Martin on the Hill, Scarborough. It bears the verse:

'Be Thou Faithful unto Death and I Will Give to Thee a Crown of Life.'

There is also an altar set at St. Augustine's Church in Grimsby that is in memory of James. There is an additional monument to James Moody in Woodland cemetery, Scarborough, the existence of which was known only to a few members of the Moody family. The headstone refers to his role in the TITANIC disaster, and commemorates Moody's sacrifice with the words:

'Greater love hath no man than this,
That a man lay down his life for his friends.'

It was long forgotten, but a recent article in the Yorkshire Post highlighted the poor condition of the memorial. It was badly overgrown and the commemorative cross had been broken off.

Air Chief-Marshal Sir Richard Edmund Charles Peirse, KCB, DSO, AFC. (1905-07)

The son of Admiral Peirse. Educated at Monkton Combe, Bath, HMS CONWAY and King's College, London.

He was Deputy Director of Operations and Intelligence during the Great War. From 1930 to 1933 he was AOC British Forces in Palestine and Transjordan. He became Deputy Chief of the Air Staff between 1933-1936, before promotion to Vice-Chief of Air Staff (1937-1940). He was AOC Bomber Command, 1940-1942; AOC-in-Chief India, 1942-1943; Allied Air C-in-C, South East Asia Command, 1943-1944. He retired in 1945.

Admiral Sir Mark C T Pizey, GBE, CB, DSO, DL. (1912-15)

He was one of the Navy's finest destroyer Captains. He was mentioned twice in despatches in 1941 and was awarded a DSO in 1942. That year he was also awarded a Bar to his DSO.

In 1951 he was appointed to be C-in-C of the Royal Indian Navy and Chairman of the Indian Chiefs of Staff. In 1953 he was appointed KBE and in 1957 GBE. His last appointment with the RN was as C-in-C Plymouth. He was made an Honorary Vice-President of The Conway Club in 1993, but died shortly thereafter. He presented the gavel and base used by the Club President.

Rear-Admiral Neil E Rankin, CB, CBE. (1955-58)

Born 24 December 1940 and raised in East Lothian,

he joined the Britannia Royal Naval College in 1959, having previously been educated at Melville College, Clifton Hall, North Berwick High School and HMS CONWAY.

Qualified both fixed and rotary wing pilot, a varied career ashore and afloat included being the first Fleet Air Arm pilot to fly the Harrier aircraft. He commanded HMS ACHILLES, HMS BACCHANTE, HMS ANDROMEDA, the Eighth Frigate Squadron and HMS ARK ROYAL. Rankin retired as Flag Officer Portsmouth, having also held tri-Service command in the Falkland Islands as a Rear-Admiral. He represented the Royal Navy at rugby, sailing and golf.

After leaving the service he was Chairman of Caledonian MacBrayne Ltd for three years between 1996 and 1999. He later became Chairman of Scottish Environment LINK.

J C Kelly Rogers, OBE, FRAeS. (1919-21)

Pilot of the first British transatlantic air service using flying boats. They had to carry so much fuel that passengers could not be carried and loads were limited to mail. The Foyles, Ireland to Botwood, Newfoundland leg of the journey took over 19 hours! In spring 1941, he took delivery of the first Boeing 314A flying boat … the largest plane in the world at the time, and flew across America via New York to Shannon.

From then on a regular wartime service was introduced and he carried many VIPs including Winston Churchill on several occasions.

Sir Arthur Henry Rostron, CBE, KBE, RD, RNR. (1885-6)

Arthur Rostron was born in Astley Bridge, Bolton, England to James and Nancy Rostron. Educated at the Bolton School from 1882 to 1883 and the Astley Bridge High School, Rostron joined CONWAY at the age of thirteen. After two years of training, he was apprenticed to the Waverley Line of Messrs. Williamson Milligan. He joined Cunard in 1895.

He is best known as the Master of CARPATHIA and rescuer of nearly seven hundred TITANIC survivors on the morning of April 15th 1912. As the result of his efforts to reach the TITANIC before it sank, and his preparations for and the conduct of the rescue of the survivors, Captain Rostron was lionised as a hero. Rostron testified about the events the night the TITANIC sank at both the US Senate enquiry into the disaster and the British Board of Trade's enquiry. TITANIC survivors, including Margaret Brown, presented Rostron with a silver cup and gold medal for his efforts the night TITANIC sank.

He went on to become Master of MAURETANIA and holder of the Blue Riband for the west-east Atlantic crossing. After World War I, he was appointed Knight Commander of the Order of the British Empire. He was made the Commodore of the Cunard fleet before retiring in 1931.

Captain Rostron is incorrectly stated in many books to have been awarded the Congressional Medal of Honor. The error is found even in works by American authors, whom one hopes would be more familiar with their nation's highest military award. In fact, Rostron was not eligible for the award, nor had he done anything worthy of it. The Congressional Medal of Honor is reserved for persons of any nationality serving in the armed forces of the United States. What Captain Rostron received was a Congressional Gold Medal. This award dates from 1776 and the first recipient was George Washington. Each medal is awarded by its own individual Act of Congress and must be ratified by the President. Early medals were generally awarded for military valour, but after the establishment of the Congressional Medal of Honor in 1865, the award was extended to all manner of persons recognised as worthy. Recipients are as varied as Thomas Edison, Walt Disney, Aaron Copland, Nelson Mandela and Frank Sinatra. The medals are of solid gold and bear on the obverse an image of the recipient. The reverse contains an image related to the action that merited the award. Rostron's medal was designed by John Flanagan, an American sculptor. Captain Rostron's award was proposed in the Senate on 28th May 1912 and was approved by a Joint Resolution of both Houses of Congress on 6th July. He was not the first British Captain to be so honoured. That distinction belongs to Captain Creighton, who in 1866 was recognised for his role in the rescue of some five hundred people from the wreck of the American steamer SAN FRANCISCO. By the time he published his memoirs in 1931, Rostron was referring to his award as the Congressional Medal of Honour (sic) and this is probably the origin of the confusion. President William Taft presented Sir Arthur's Gold medal on March 1st 1913 at the White House. Taft had lost the 1912 election, but in those days the outgoing President did not retire until March 4th.

Captain Rostron was also awarded the American Cross of Honor. This decoration was given by the Society of the American Cross of Honor, an organisation devoted to recognising bravery in the saving of life in non-military situations. The medal was frequently awarded for rescues at sea. There was also British involvement and the gold version of the decoration was sometimes awarded on the recommendation of the Royal National Lifeboat Institution. This is probably the reason for the medal being presented to Captain Rostron at the British Embassy, also on March 1st 1913. He was also awarded a medal from the Liverpool Shipwreck and Humane Society and a gold medal from the Shipwreck Society of New York.

Vice-Admiral Sir C W R Royds. (1890-92)

Scott's First Officer on the RMS DISCOVERY during his first Antarctic Expedition. Cape Royds is named after him and is also the location of Shackleton's hut. After a long naval career he went on to become Commissioner of the Metropolitan Police. There is a tablet to his memory in Brompton Parish Church.

Kenneth Shoesmith. (1906-08)

Kenneth was born in Halifax in Yorkshire, grew up in Blackpool. Despite showing early artistic talent, he decided on a career at sea and became a CONWAY Cadet. After CONWAY he joined the Royal Mail Line, but continued his enthusiasm for drawing and painting. He was mainly self-taught, but did take a correspondence course early in his career. Like many artists, his style changed considerably during his life. In his early years, he had a natural flowing style, but he developed a more 'Art Deco' style later.

At some point he left the sea and between the wars he worked for the publishers Thomas Forman. They produced all Cunard's postcards and Shoesmith created many very well known images for them. He also designed posters for a number of other companies, including the Royal Mail Line. OCs will know him best for his illustration that graces the cover of Masefield's 'The CONWAY' and for his beautiful picture 'The Training Ship CONWAY at Rock Ferry in the Mersey'. He painted the First War Honours Board which hangs in Birkenhead Priory.

He was a prolific artist and his works included several large pieces for the old QUEEN MARY, including 'The Madonna of the Atlantic' for the Cabin Class Drawing Room. He also produced the screen of harbour scenes. These are still on display in the QUEEN MARY at Long Beach, California.

He was famous for his marine posters advertising pre-war Trans-Atlantic Liners. His style of representing ocean liners became instantly recognisable and is still copied to this day. A collection of over three hundred items of his work is in the Ulster Museum, Belfast, Northern Ireland.

David Reynolds wrote a book about him 'Kenneth Shoesmith and Royal Mail'.

Captain David Smith. RN. (1942-44)

Patron of the Conway Club, Elder Brother of Trinity House, and former Warden and Chief Executive. Longest serving Conway Club Committee Member, over 50 years. Longest serving President of the Conway Club … over ten years.

Iain Duncan Smith. (1968-72)

Iain Duncan Smith was born in April 1954. He joined CONWAY in January 1968 when he was nearly 14. During his sojourn he was a foc'sleman, a drummer in the band, captain of the cricket team in 1972, won 'colours' in the first XV in the Autumn 1971 term and played for the hockey team. He won the Lawrence Holt prize for History in 1972 and left with 3 A levels and 8 O levels.

From CONWAY he went on to Perugia University in Italy, then to Sandhurst and so to the Scots Guards, with whom he served from 1975 to 81. He then retired from the Army and went into industry. He was a Director of GEC/Marconi from 1981-88; a Director of Bellwinch Pic from 1988-89 and Publishing Director of Jane's Information Group from 1989-92.

He contested Bradford West in the 1987 General Election. He was Vice-Chairman of Fulham Conservative Association in 1991. The following year he was elected Member of Parliament for Chingford. He sat on the Standards in Public Life (Nolan) Select Committee and the Members' Interests Select Committee. He was a member of the Administration Select Committee and a former member of the Health Select Committee. From 1992-97 he was secretary of the Conservative Back Bench Foreign and Commonwealth Affairs Committee and a member of the Conservative Back Bench Defence Committee. He was also on the Conservative Central Office General Election Campaign Team. Following boundary changes he was elected Member of Parliament for Chingford and Woodford Green in May 1997 with a majority of 5,714. From June 1997 he was Shadow Secretary of State for Social Security. In June 1999 he was appointed Shadow Secretary of State for Defence. He led the Conservative Party from 2001 to 2003.

Blair Hughes-Stanton. (1915–17)

A painter, wood engraver, draughtsman and teacher; born in London, son of painter Sir Herbert Hughes-Stanton, President of the Royal Society of Painters in Watercolours. He was educated at Colet Court and joined CONWAY at thirteen. Unable to master spelling and punctuation and after failing to get into the Royal Navy, he studied art … first at the Byam Shaw School (1919-22), then the Leon Underwood School of Painting and Sculpture, and then in the Royal Academy School. At Underwood's school he met Henry Moore and they formed a group including Eileen Agar, Gertrude Hermes and Ralph Chubb. In 1925 the group broke away from the Society of Wood Engravers and formed the English Wood Engravers Society. Hughes-Stanton married Gertrude Hermes in 1926. He succeeded John Maynard as head of the Gregynog Press in 1931 and with his second wife, Ida Graves, established the Gemini Press. He won an international prize for engraving at the Venice Biennale in 1938. During the war he worked in camouflage with the Royal Engineers, afterwards he was sent to Greece (he was captured, became a POW and was shot in the face). After the war, commissions for private press books dried up and his war wound seriously affected his three-dimensional vision. He found work teaching at Westminster School of Art 1947-8 and from 1948 Hughes-Stanton was a lecturer in printmaking and drawing at the Society of Wood Engravers, St. Martins and The Central School of Art. He latterly lived in Manningtree, Essex. His wood engravings were the subject of a book, 'The Wood Engravings of Blair Hughes-Stanton' by Penelope Hughes-Stanton.

Captain Donald Stewart. (1920s)

In 1944 he was on the Blue Funnel ship, AUTOMEDON when it was raided and subsequently sunk. After the other Officers were killed, he played a key part in trying to stop the Germans finding important secret documents, which ultimately led to the bombing of Pearl Harbour.

Ken Strange. (1937-39)

At seventeen, just before World War Two, Ken finished two years in Conway and moved to the USA where the US Navy sent him to Officer's training at Swarthmore. He shipped out on the USS RANGER, which patrolled the North African coast, and, at 20, was made Chief Ordnance Officer on the USS INTREPID. During his tour of duty, the INTREPID and its crew survived a kamikaze attack in the South Pacific, returning on its own to San Francisco for repairs.

He returned from WWII a changed man. Though he had physically survived the war, he was spiritually wounded. It was his Uncle Ernest, who loved him like a son, who urged him to pursue his art. Ken applied and was accepted into the Boston Museum School. Raoul Dufy and his explorations of colour and line were his greatest influence. His Seagulls painted in 1964 will have a special resonance for OCs.

Group Captain T Q Studd, DL, DFC. (1909-11)

His achievements were very special … CONWAY Cadet Captain, Gold Medallist, commissioned Officer in all three services. He was the first person to fly from North Wales to Ireland. His flying licence number was No. 50 in RFC. An interesting side line, he taught Douglas Bader to fly!

Captain L J Thompson. (1939-41)

Bowman of the No 1 Motor Boat that rescued the 45 crew from the SS TACOMA CITY which was blown up by a magnetic mine in the Mersey near the CONWAY in March 1941. During his voyage at the age of 18 on the Blue Star MV DUNEDIN STAR, he was shipwrecked and rescued from the notorious Skeleton Coast in SW Africa. These exploits are covered in the book and film 'Skeleton Coast'. In 2000 he published his own account of the adventure entitled 'The Loss of a Ship'. He served twice as President of the Conway Club, between 1986-90 and 1992-96, and has been chairman of the HMS CONWAY Trust from 1988 to 2005.

Captain W E 'Bil' Warwick, CBE, RD, RNR. (1926-28)

First Master of the QE II and previous Master of the QUEEN ELIZABETH and the QUEEN MARY. Subsequently became Commodore of Cunard Line. Bil was the father of Captain Ron Warwick.

Captain W E 'Ron' Warwick. (1956-57)

Recently retired as Commodore of Cunard and first Captain of the new QUEEN MARY II.

Captain Matthew 'Chummy' Webb. (1860-62)

After CONWAY he served a three-year apprenticeship with Rathbone Brothers of Liverpool. Whilst serving as Second Mate on the Cunard ship, RUSSIA, travelling from New York to Liverpool, he attempted to rescue a man overboard by diving into the sea in mid-Atlantic. The man was never found, but Webb's daring won him an award of £100 and the Stanhope Gold Medal, and made him a hero of the British press.

In 1873, Webb was serving as Captain of the steamship EMERALD when he read an account of the failed attempt by J Johnson to swim the English Channel. He became inspired to try himself, and left his job to begin training, first at Lambeth Baths, then in the cold waters of the Thames and the English Channel. Webb was the first man to swim the Channel from England to France. The route from France to England had much more favourable tides and so had been swum many times. Webb's route was much more difficult. It is estimated that with tidal drift he swam approximately fifty miles. He swam in his red CONWAY bathing shorts.

After many other long distance races and endurance swims over many years, he died attempting to swim the rapids below Niagara Falls. At CONWAY he was regarded as a long distance or endurance swimmer rather than a racer. The Captain Webb Memorial Shield was competed for annually by Cadets.

Sir Clive R Woodward. (1969-74)

Coach of the England Rugby Union team, previously an international rugby player. He was awarded the OBE in June 2003. He was knighted in 2004 for his services to rugby after England won the Rugby World Cup

Vice-Admiral Sir Peter Woodhead. (1954-57)

Vice-Admiral Sir Peter Woodhead served in the Royal Navy until 1994, including 15 years as a Fleet Air Arm pilot, command of four ships and the appointment of Chief of Staff to the Joint Service Commander of the Falklands Task Force during the 1982 conflict. Subsequently he served as a Squadron Commander, Director of Naval Operations, Captain of an Aircraft Carrier and, as an Admiral, commanded both the 1st and 2nd Flotillas. His final appointment in the Navy was as the Deputy Supreme Allied Commander Atlantic.

On leaving the Navy he was appointed as the first Prisons Ombudsman from 1994 to 2000. He is currently Deputy Chairman of a technology company, a member of the Security Vetting Appeals Panel at the Cabinet Office, a Lay Preacher and is involved in eight charities primarily in the field of Crime Reduction and Homelessness. He was appointed to the Armed Forces' Pay Review Body in 2002.

HMS CONWAY SENIOR OFFICERS

NAVY

Vice-Admiral D S **Boyle,** RCN. (1939-40)
Vice-Admiral Sir David **Brown,** KCB. (1941-45) Former Flag Officer, Plymouth. The last Flag Officer of the Royal Navy to have served afloat in a ship of the line.
Vice-Admiral Leslie Newton **Brownfield,** CB, CBI. (1915-17) Naval Attache to Thailand 1939-41, commanded battleship RAMILIES, later President of the Admiralty Interview Board, Admiral Superintendent Devonport.
Vice-Admiral **Carden.** (1869-71)
Vice-Admiral Sir David **Clutterbuck,** KBE, CB. (1926-29) Deputy Supreme Allied Commander North Atlantic during Second World War.

Admiral **Collins**. No details

Vice-Admiral Sir Archibald **Day,** KBE, CB, DSO. (1913-14). Hydrographer of the Navy, 1950-55.

Vice-Admiral Thomas Bernard **Drew**, CB, OBE. (1902 03) Awarded OBE in WW1 for pursuit of GOEBEN and BRESLAU in the light cruiser GLOUCESTER.

Rear-Admiral J P **Edwards**, CB, LVO. (1942-44)

Rear-Admiral Douglas Henry **Everett**, CB, CBE, MBE, DSO. (1911-13)

Admiral **Franklin**. Cheating a little … he was CONWAY's fourth Captain Superintendent, promoted on retirement.

Commodore C G **Greenfield**. (1943-45)

Commodore Henry Robertson **Lane**, RNR. A Marine Superintendent of Cunard and ADC to King George V1 in 1951.

Commodore D T **Marr**, RN, DSC. (1922-24)

Rear-Admiral C B **Mayo**, RN, CB, CBE. (1923-25)

Rear-Admiral G D **Moore**, CBE, OBE, RAN. (1910-12)

Vice-Admiral Sir Charles E **Morgan**, KBE, CB, DSO, RN, (1902-5)

Commodore M B **Morrow**, RCN. (1937-39)

Admiral **Murray**, RN.

Admiral H S F **Niblett**. (1896)

Admiral Sir Richard **Peirse**, KCB, KBE, RN. (1873-75) He invented the Gunnery Control System for the Royal Navy used in all capital ships with large guns.

Admiral Sir Mark **Pizey**, RAN. (1912-15)

Rear-Admiral N E **Rankin**, CB, CBE. (1955-58) The last Flag Officer Portsmouth. The appointment is now held by a Commodore.

Admiral A R **Rattray**, RIN, CB, KBE. (1906-08)

Vice-Admiral Sir C W R **Royds.** (1890-92)
Commodore J F **Ruthven**, FRGS, RNR. (1864-65)
Admiral Sir **Sackville-Carden**. (1869-70)
Rear-Admiral K M **Saul**, RNZN, CB. (1942-44)
Rear-Admiral R W **Timbrell**, CF, DSC, CD, RCN. (1935-37)
Vice-Admiral Sir Peter **Woodhead.** (1954-57) Deputy
Supreme Commander Atlantic.

ARMY
Major-General G W **Barber**, CB, CMC, DSO. (Australian
Army). (1882-84)
Hon. Brigadier-General, Captain Robert Herbert Wilfred
Hughes, CB, CSI, CMG, DSO, RD. (1885-6)
Brigadier-General G **Nicholson**. (1907-09)

AIR FORCE
Air Chief Marshal Sir Richard Edmund Charles **Peirse,**
KCB, DSO, AFC. (1905-07)
Air Commodore David Neal **Roberts.** AFC. (1920-22)
Air Commodore Fred **Rump**. (1927-29)
Air Marshall **Worthington** (Years not known)
Air Vice Marshall Sir William M **Yool**, CB, CBE. 1908-10)

HMS CONWAY
International Sportsmen

John Bligh (1966-69) Rugby (schoolboy), England.

D G Chapman (1922-24) Represented Great Britain in the 4 by 400 m at the 1928 Amsterdam Olympics.

Walter Elliot Imp (Years not known) Rugby, England.

Dai Phillips (1968-71) Rugby, Wales.

Padre E Turner ran the Marathon for Great Britain in the London Olympic Games.

AT Young Scrum Half for England RUFC throughout 1924.

Sir Clive Woodward (1969-74) Rugby, England.

CHAPTER FOUR

CADET SCHOOL SHIP HMS CONWAY WORLD WAR ONE HONOURS

Foreword

The lists of honours awarded to former Cadets of HMS Conway during World Wars One and Two are now located in a dedicated chapel in the Birkenhead Priory together with three Memorial boards listing those who lost their lives in those conflicts. Initials and names are simply listed alphabetically under each award; no other details about events so many years ago: how they lost their lives, or what they did to be honoured with an award.

Information about those who are listed is limited and scattered: old copies of The Cadet magazine, records held in the Liverpool Maritime Museum, War Memorials, and other, often obscure, sources. However, the advent of internet search facilities has provided the impetus to find out a little more about the names.

A former Cadet, Geoffrey L Haskins, who was in the Ship, 1940-1943, has taken on the task accessing records both official and unofficial. The main ones which he wishes to acknowledge are:

Official sources:
Commonwealth War Graves Commission.
London Gazette.

Unofficial sources:

Naval-History.net (www.naval-history.net): a comprehensive compilation of Admiralty casualty reports, daily and monthly dispositions of British and Commonwealth naval vessels, all created by enthusiasts including Don Kindell, a US researcher, Gordon Smith, an author, and Geoffrey Mason, a retired RN officer among other contributors.

U-boat.net (www.uboat.net/lndex): owned and organised by Gudmundur Hergason of Iceland who has access to a remarkably wide selection of enthusiastic and knowledgeable contributors.

World War Two unit histories and officers (www.unithistories. com): An ambitious project with useful data on the awards to officers and their wartime careers. Owned by Hans Houterman and Jeroen Koppes of the Netherlands.

The Minewarfare and Clearance Diving Officers' Association (www.mcdoa.org.uk): Excellent lists of all awards made in WW Two in respect of minelaying, mine sweeping and bomb and mine disposal.

Awards to the Royal Canadian Navy (www.rcnvr.com): a comprehensive listing of all Canadian Naval and Merchant Navy recipients of honours.

There is a plethora of other sites that come to light when searching … Museums, Shipping Companies, Service Associations and the BBC archives. All are available in the public domain and can be rewarding. Some anomalies have been found along the way: differences in spelling of names, possible mis-identifications by Conway's original compiler of the records, and some names that defy all attempts to find any information at all. The London Gazette in particular, although a magnificent set of records, is not easy to research; its tricks have to be mastered, and barriers overcome!

Finally, the compiler ... Geoffrey L Haskins (1940-43) wishes it to be known that he has received much help and encouragement from other members of the Conway Club: John Southwood (1955-57), who is the expert on Conway records in the Liverpool Maritime Museum, Haydn Lockwood (1946-47) of the NW Branch who provides encouragement when spirits lag, Messrs Dave Donaldson (1959-60), Mike Sanders (1958-60) and Rob Tubb (1967-70) have assisted nobly with some of the searching. Finally, his long suffering wife, a native of Menai Bridge, deserves appreciation as she so patiently put up with his obsession with 'lists'.

All entries are made in good faith but have not been fully checked, edited, reviewed (peer or otherwise) and are not guaranteed to be accurate. Any comments, suggestions or additional information is welcome. The compiler hopes those subjects who have 'crossed the bar' would have approved the results of this study which has been completed as a mark of respect.

HMS CONWAY HONOURS WWI

ACHESON (Albert Edward). CONWAY 1877/79. Commander, RN.

OBE: 4/6/18.

CBE: 4/7/19. In recognition of services as Royal Naval Transport Officer in Manchester during the war. Royal Naval Transport Service.

ALLEN (Reginald). CONWAY 1914/15. Sub-Lieutenant, RNR.

DSC: 14/3/16. For services performed under shell fire on the beaches and in steam boats off the beaches in the Dardenelles.

BAR to DSC: 16/11/17. For services in action against enemy submarines.

APPLEYARD (Sydney Vere). CONWAY 1897/99. Major, Army Medical Corps, Australian.

DSO: As two dates were given … 16/11/17 and 19/3/18 … so it is possible that he was awarded a BAR to DSO. 'On the Western Front he established a forward dressing station immediately at rear of the front line during an attack, and attended continuously to the wounded, frequently going out and dressing cases in the open, under heavy shell fire ... his fearlessness was an inspiration.'

BAIRNSFATHER (George Edward). CONWAY 1868/70. Captain, RN.

CBE: 4/6/18. Divisional Naval Transport Officer, Dover

BALFOUR (Alfred Stevenson).   CONWAY 1884/86. Captain, RIM.

OBE. Nothing is known except that he entered service from CONWAY to serve in India.

BARKER (Henry Pinder). CONWAY 1898/99.

DSC. No further information.

BARNISH (Geoffrey Howard). CONWAY NK. Lieutenant, RNR.

DSO: 13/9/18. For services involving enemy submarines.

BARRADELL (Lancelot Harris). CONWAY NK. Sub-Lieutenant, RNR.

LEGION OF HONOUR, (CROIS DE CHEVALIER): 15/9/16. Presented by the President of the French Republic following the Battle of Jutland, 31/5/16.

BATE (Francis William). CONWAY NK. Commander, RD, RNR.

OBE: 24/6/19.   For valuable services as Assistant Transport Officer and as District Superintendent of Ship Repairs in Southampton.

BATTLE (Walter Cyprian). CONWAY 1896/98. Lieutenant, RNR.

DSO: 14/5/18. For services on the Mediterranean Station.

BEEVOR (Miles).   CONWAY NK.   Major, Temporary Lieutenant-Colonel, Army.

DSO: 30/5/19. He seems to have been a Battalion Commander on the Western Front and on HQ Staff, East Kent Regiment.

BELL (Richard Logesdaile). CONWAY 1911/12. Second-Lieutenant, Army.

MC. The Cadet quotes: 'For conspicuous gallantry and devotion to duty whilst with a party constructing roads. From a hill in front of him sudden bursts of enemy rifle fire made him apprehensive for the safety of a party of sappers working on the enemy side.' He served in the Hampshire Regiment in the Middle East. He was Killed in Action, 1918, and buried in Ramleh War Cemetery, Palestine.

BENT (Philip Eric). CONWAY 1910/12. Lieutenant-Colonel, Army.

DSO: after 1916. Several Gazettes chart his progress to Lieutenant-Colonel, but the one gazetting his DSO is elusive. He served in the 9th Battalion, Bedfordshire Regiment in Belgium. He was killed in action in France, 1918. He joined the Army as a Private in 1914, disguising his possession of a Second Mates Certificate. Bent was a native of Halifax, Nova Scotia.

VICTORIA CROSS. 2/3/1918. Details of this award are found in the opening pages of this book. Coolness and a magnificent example shown to all ranks by Lieutenant-Colonel Bent resulted in the securing of portion of the line. "Come on the Tigers!"

BERESFORD (Charles Frederick). CONWAY 1895/97. Flying Officer, RAF.

MBE: 26/11/24. There are no details. Flying Officer

Charles Frederick Beresford Bassil, RAF, was placed on the Retired List due to ill health.

BONNER (Charles George). CONWAY 1899/1901. Lieutenant, RNR.

DSC: 20/7/17. For services in action with enemy submarines.

VICTORIA CROSS. 6/10/1917. Details of this award are found in the opening pages of this book.

BRADLEY (John P). CONWAY NK. Lieutenant, RNR.

DSC: 21/9/17. Gazette has verbatim report from Captain Wilfred Nunn, Commanding Officer of the Tigris Flotilla. Report reads 'Lieutenant Bradley did very good work by taking a captured Turkish steamer down river to Basra with enemy wounded'. Citation: 'For coolness under fire on all occasions'. Bradley was aboard HMS TARANTULA (a river gunboat) and was involved in the campaign to capture and occupy Baghdad, Mesopotamia (December 1916 – March 1917).

BRAY (Paul Dudley). CONWAY 1887/89. Customs Officer.

OBE: 27/6/19. Bray was a Customs Officer in Durban, South Africa.

BROOKE-SMITH, (Reginald John). CONWAY NK. Lieutenant, RN.

DSC: 16/4/18. In recognition of services in submarines. He was transferred from Lieutenant, RNR, to Lieutenant, RN, on 8/3/18 'for gallantry in action'.

BUCKLEY (William Smith). CONWAY 1912/14. Acting Sub-Lieutenant, RNR.

DSC: 8/4/19. For service in Local Defence Flotillas, 1ˢᵗ July to 11ᵗʰ November, 1918 in home waters.

BUCKNALL (Rixon). CONWAY 1917/19. Lieutenant, Army.

MBE: 31/5/29. Described as Attached Staff (Special Appointment Class GG), North China Command, Coldstream Guards.

BULLOCK (Charles Arthur). CONWAY 1891/92. Lieutenant-Commander, RD, RNR.

OBE: 12/9/19. For valuable services in command of HM Cable Trawler, SIALKOT.

CAMPBELL (Charles Ross). CONWAY 1890/92. Temporary Lieutenant-Colonel, Acting Captain, RIM.

DSO: 23/8/18. There is a long list of awards and promotions: 'for distinguished service in connection with military operations in Mesopotamia'. He served with the Royal Engineers.

MVO when he held the rank of Commander, (Acting Captain), RIM, and was Presidency Port Officer (1924). He served 24 years in the RIM.

CAMPBELL (Donald). CONWAY 1888/90. Acting Commander, RN.

OBE: 4/6/18. He was a Port Coaling Officer and that is all that is known.

CAMPBELL (John Duncan). CONWAY 1902/03. Commander, RN.

DSC: 21/3/19. For services in minesweeping from 1ˢᵗ July to 31ˢᵗ December, 1918.

DSO. This listing may be in error, the DSO is not mentioned in post war Gazettes. Lieutenant-Commander J D Campbell was placed on the Retired List with rank of Commander, 6/9/31. It is also possible that he was awarded an OBE, 29/12/31.

CARDEN (Sackville Hamilton). CONWAY 1869/71. Vice-Admiral, RN.

KCMG: 30/3/05. He carried his flag in HMS QUEEN ELIZABETH at the Dardenelles. He died in 1930.

CASEY (Denis A) CONWAY NK. Acting Lieutenant, RNR.

DSC: 24/10/16. In recognition of services in submarines in enemy waters.

CHARTER (William Forster). CONWAY 1908/09. Second-Lieutenant, Army.

MC: 24/8/17. For conspicuous gallantry and devotion to duty. His company formed part of a working party two hundred yards from enemy lines. His coolness and disregard for danger contributed very largely to the orderly nature of the withdrawal whereby many casualties were avoided. Charter served with the Scottish Rifles in France and Belgium.

CHATER (John D G). CONWAY 1912/13. Lieutenant, RNR.

DSC. Two gazettes show him promoted to Sub-Lieutenant 28/8/16 and Lieutenant 25/6/18.

CHEETHAM (Herbert Charles Valentine). CONWAY NK. Commander, RD, RNR.

DSO: 29/12/16. He was a Chief Transport Officer. Performed exceptional service under heavy fire during attacks on Jabassi on 8th October, 1914 and the subsequent retirement downstream after dark. He commanded the advance detachment of the Nyong Flotilla on the Edea expedition which enabled the French troops to land without opposition. Cheetham served in the Cameroons Expeditionary Force in West Africa. He is not listed as having served in CONWAY as a Cadet, but may have been a staff member.

COX (Bernard T). CONWAY NK. Lieutenant, RNR.

DSO: 29/3/05. This gazette contains the reports of Vice-Admirals Carden (1869-71) and de Robeck on the events of the British and French Squadrons against the defences of the Dardenelles. Part of the report is a list of personnel who are recommended for awards and promotions, among these is Lieutenant B T Cox. Cox served in HMS PRINCE GEORGE in the Dardenelles.

CRAVEN (John). CONWAY 1885/87. Merchant Navy.

OBE. He may have been one of the few WW One Merchant Navy awards, but nothing found 1900-1930. He received the King's Gold Medal 1887 in CONWAY.

CREASE (Thomas Evans). CONWAY 1888/90. Acting Captain, RN.

CBE. Awarded before 1916.

CB: 2/6/16. Awarded for services rendered during the war.

ORDER OF THE RISING SUN.

CROIX DE GUERRE.

LEGION D' HONNEUR.

He had at his own request been put on the retired list in 1910, but obviously returned to service. Apparently, Crease was much involved with political and diplomatic matters in the Mediterranean.

CUSTANCE (Frederick H M). CONWAY NK. Acting Captain, RD, RNR.

DSO: 29/4/19.

CUTHBERT (J)). CONWAY NK. Captain.

MC.

BAR to MC. There are several gazettes detailing Captain Cuthbert's movements in 1918-20, but the awards are hard to uncover. Cuthbert obviously had an active war, but no other information can be found.

DAVIES (Bertram Harold). CONWAY 1899/1901. Lieutenant, RNR.

MiD: 18/6/18. For services in Patrol Cruisers from 1st January to 31st December, 1917. These Patrol Cruisers probably came to be termed Armed Merchant Cruisers.

OBE. Davies was awarded an OBE and finally the RD in 1922.

de BALINHARD (John Carnegyde). CONWAY NK. Acting Lieutenant-Colonel.

DSO: 1/1/19. Gazette 31266 lists him as having the DSO and other later Gazettes show him as a confirmed Major in the Regular Canadian Army, the Saskatchewan Regiment.

de CAEN (Raymond George Francis Herault). CONWAY 1898/1900. Lieutenant, RN.

DSC: 8/4/19. Awarded for services in sloops employed on convoy, escort and patrol duties between 1/8/18 and 11/11/18.

de WET (Eric Oloff). CONWAY 1909/10. Sub-Lieutenant, RN.

DSC: 13/8/15. In the same Gazette as Edward Unwin won his Victoria Cross. Eric de Wet was one of the Midshipmen manning the small craft during the action. He was promoted to Sub-Lieutenant on 15/11/16. He was serving in HMS LONDON in the Dardenelles, Gallipoli campaign. He lost his life in HMS NARBOROUGH when she was wrecked at Scapa Flow, 12/1/18.

DIXON (Alan). CONWAY 1894/96. Commander, RN.

OBE: 27/6/19. For valuable services as Resident Senior Naval Officer, Smyrna since the Armistice.

DONOVAN (Edgar C M). CONWAY 1899/01. Sub-Lieutenant, RNVR.

CROIX DE GUERRE WITH PALMS, (France). He served with the Royal Artillery Seige Guns. Donovan was killed on the 26th April, 1917 and was buried in Coxyde Military Cemetery, Belgium.

DREW (Harold). CONWAY 1809/10. Sub-Lieutenant, RN.

DSC: 11/5/17. A generic citation was in common use … 'For Miscellaneous Services'.

DREW (Thomas Bernard). CONWAY 1902/04. Lieutenant-Commander, RN.

OBE: 15/7/19. For valuable services in HMS REVENGE, 1ˢᵗ Battle Squadron.

DRURY (Edward Dumerque). CONWAY 1895/96. Lieutenant-Commander, RNR.

OBE: 1/1/19. He commanded HMS EMPRESS, (ex-Channel Ferry), a Sea Plane tender in the Eastern Mediteranean. Drury received the CONWAY King's Gold Medal in 1896.

DUFF (Douglas Valder). CONWAY 1914/15. Merchant Navy, RNR.

MiD. RMS THRACIA (Cunard) was torpedoed in Bay of Biscay 27ᵗʰ March, 1917. Duff was rescued by a French ship, L'ORIENT and was the sole survivor. This may not be the event leading to a 'Foreign' award. Duff went back to sea in the RNR. WW Two Honours Board contains references to his MiD and the CONWAY web-site has a brief biography of this notable and adventurous author and OC.

ELDERTON (Ferdinand Halford). CONWAY 1879/81. Captain, RIM.

DSO: 29/11/00. In recognition of services during recent operations in China, a number of persons are listed, Elderton included. There is a Report of Proceedings by Lieutenant-General Sir Alfred Gaselee, Commanding Officer of the British Contingent, China Expeditionary Force. Elderton is mentioned in connection with 'sea and river transport'. The campaign was concerned with the Boxer Rebellion.

CMG: 28/12/17. For valuable services rendered during the War. Elderton retired as Captain, DSO, CMG, RIM.
ELLIOT. OBE. No further details.

EVANS (Benjamin). CONWAY 1912/14. Lieutenant, RNR.
MiD: 18/12/17. For services in action with submarines.
DSC. The gazette for his DSC has not been found, but he was promoted as Lieutenant, DSC, on 28/1/19.

EVERETT (Douglas Henry). CONWAY 1911/13. Sub-Lieutenant, RN.
MBE: 17/7/19. For valuable services in HMS RESOLUTION, 1ˢᵗ Battle Squadron.

FAREWELL (Michael Warren). CONWAY 1883/85. Commander, RIM.
CIE: 31/12/15. There is no particular citation. He had been in the RIM for thirty years by 1915 and was a Port Officer and Marine Transport Officer in Karachi.

FARR (Edward Douglas). CONWAY NK. Acting Major, RE.
MC: 13/9/18. This is a long Gazette of 206 pages of awards to Officers and Warrant Officers. Farr's citation reads: 'For conspicuous gallantry and devotion to duty during enemy attacks. As Officer Commanding Inland Water Transport, he supervised the evacuation of craft and materials, patrolling the river for many hours by day and night under severe enemy shell fire.' This was probably in France or Belgium after the German Spring offensive.

FOLEY (Reginald Hubert). CONWAY NK. Lieutenant, RNVR.

DSC: 16/4/18. For services in Auxiliary Patrol, Mineweeping, or Coastal Motor Boats from 01/1/18 to 30/6/18.

MiD: 17/9/18. For services in Minesweeping from 1/4/17 to 31/12/17. His activities were all in European waters.

FREEMAN (John Richard Dudley). CONWAY 1909/12. Acting Lieutenant, RN.

DSC. Gallantly performed his duty in charge of a 4-inch gun while in action against superior forces whilst serving in HMS MARY ROSE.

FRITH (William Willoughby Cole). CONWAY 1890/92. Commander, RNR.

OBE: 28/3/19. For valuable services as Chief Examination Officer in the Tyne.

FURNIVAL (Horace William). CONWAY 1910/12. Sub-Lieutenant, RNR.

DSC: 20/8/16. In recognition of his services as an aeroplane observer and continuous good work while attached to a Wing of the RNAS at Dunkirk.

GARSTIN (Richard Hart). CONWAY 1900-02. Acting Temporary Lieutenant-Colonel.

OBE: 15/11/18. He served in Italy with Inland Water Transport, but was awarded his OBE for distinguished service in connection with military operations in Mesopotamia. When he left CONWAY he joined the RIM and then transferred into the RE as an Inland Waterway expert.

CBE. In WW Two he was a Commodore, RNR, Commodore of Ocean Convoys, and was awarded the CBE. Garstin was Killed in Action in 1942.

GIBB (Alfred Spencer). CONWAY 1882/84. Commander, RD, RNR.

DSO: 14/7/16. Serving in the Auxiliary Patrol Service (APS) in recognition of his services in Armed Yachts, Trawlers and Drifters from 1/1/15 to 31/1/16. Gibb 'endured extremely arduous and hazardous conditions of weather and exposure to enemy attack and mines with marked zeal, gallantry and success'. He was awarded the King's Gold Medal in CONWAY in 1884.

GIBSON (Charles Mends). CONWAY 1889/91. Acting Commander, RN.

OBE: 12/9/19. For valuable services during the war.

GIBSON (William). CONWAY NK. Lieutenant-Colonel, Army.

MC: 25/8/16. For conspicuous gallantry during the capture of an enemy position in France. Though wounded, he carried up a machine gun to an important position. He was serving in the Staffordshire Regiment.

DSO: 29/11/18. There is a long citation, including: 'For conspicuous gallantry and initiative when in command of his Battalion during five days operations ... reorganised ... great skills ... pursued retreating enemy ... captured many important positions. His coolness and determination inspired his men and contributed to the success of the operation.' Gibson was serving in the 10th West Yorkshire Regiment.

During WW Two, Lieutenant-Colonel Gibson was active in the Buckinghamshire Home Guard.

GOOLD-ADAMS (Hamilton John). CONWAY 1880/83. Major, Royal Scots, Lothian Regiment.

CB: 14/1/98. He was the Resident Commissioner in the Bechuanaland Protectorate.

GCMG. Announcement that Major Sir Hamilton John Goold-Adams, GCMG, CB to be Governor of the State of Queensland. Goold-Adams was the first President of the Conway Club, 1915-1920. Died en route to UK from Australia in 1922.

GREENHILL (Joseph William). CONWAY NK. Captain, RD, RNR.

DSO. Quoted in Gazettes as holding the DSO in 1920 on promotion to Commander, RNR.

CBE: 30/6/25. Possibly awarded on retirement from seafaring later in life.

GREGORY (George). CONWAY NK. Commander, RD, RNR.

OBE. No details were found.

MiD. Gregory was twice gazetted for a MiD for operations in conjunction with military operations in Palestine from September to November, 1918.

DSO: 18/2/19. For landing stores and ammunition in Palestine, from October to December, 1917. He was Naval Transport Officer in Charge, responsible for landings on an exposed coast of Palestine and by his skill and determination contributed markedly to the success of the operation.

CBE: 1/7/19. For valuable services as Divisional Naval Transport Officer, Beirut.

GRIFFIN (Robert H). CONWAY NK. Commander, RD, RNR.

OBE: 31/1/18. It is not easy to locate the details of OBEs.

GUARD (Frederick H W). CONWAY NK. Lieutenant-Colonel, Hampshire Regiment.

DSO.

CMG. All awards dated after August 1918. Several Gazettes track him from Second Lieutenant to Lieutenant-Colonel, DSO, CMG, the awards dating after August 1918 when he commanded a Battalion of the Royal Scots.

CROIX DE GUERRE: 18/7/19. Permission granted to wear.

HADDOCK (Herbert James). CONWAY NK. Captain, RD, RNR.

CB: 24/6/02. Long list of awards to the Order of the Bath. Interesting entry referring to Captain Haddock and White Star Line. He was the first Captain of TITANIC for the delivery voyage from Belfast to Southampton.

ADC to HM the KING: 21/8/16. Captain H J Haddock, CB, RD, RNR, appointed ADC to HM the King. Haddock died in 1946.

HALL (Reginald Staunton). CONWAY 1893/95. Second Lieutenant.

DCM: 5/2/15. At this date Private Hall of the King's Hussars was promoted to Second Lieutenant. There was no mention of the DCM at that time. Served in the Dragoon Guards (Queens Bays).

HALLETT (Cecil Gwydr). 1902/04. Lieutenant, RIM.

DSC: 10/8/17. Report of Proceedings for the campaign quote: 'Has given me valuable help throughout the campaign, and has carried out the gunnery duties for the Squadron. His experience, particularly under fire, is of great value, and he has frequently done this under fire.' The DSC was awarded during the campaign to capture and occupy Baghdad December 1916 - March 1917. He served in HMS PROSERINE (Third Class Cruiser) in Mesopotamia.

DSO: 21/3/19. Appointed to a commission as Lieutenant RIM.

HAMBLY (Andrew). CONWAY NK. Commander, RN.

DSO: 5/4/18. For services in vessels of the Auxiliary Patrol, 1st January to 31st December, 1917.

HAMILTON (Anthony). CONWAY 1886/88. Commander, RIM.

DSO and MiD: 29/10/15 and 29/10/15. Both were awarded for distinguished services in the field.

HAMILTON (Leslie). CONWAY NK. Lieutenant, RFC.

DFC: 7/2/19. The gazette stated that Hamilton is a gallant and skilful scout pilot who never hesitates to attack enemy formations however superior their numbers. He has brought down, or assisted to bring down, six enemy machines in Salonika. By 1920 he had a Short Service Commission as Flying Officer, RAF.

HAROLD (Austin Edward). CONWAY 1887/89. Colonel, RIM.

DSO: 22/12/16. For distinguished service in the field in connection with military operations in Mesopotamia. He served in the Inland Waterways Directorate in Mesopotamia and had been granted commission as Captain, RIM, 21/3/19. Several gazettes track his progress in the RE to Colonel on 6/1/20.

HARRIS (George Henry). CONWAY 1867/69. Master, RNR.

OBE: 4/6/18. King's Birthday Honours refers to Lieutenant-Commander G H Harris, RNR. His Mercantile Marine Company is not mentioned. Harris must have been about 65 years of age in 1918 and due to retire. He died 21/2/29 in Lymington.

HARRIS (Stafford Berkley). CONWAY 1908/12. Flying Officer, RAF.

AFC. Reference found to S B Harris, AFC, being granted a Permanent Commission as Flying Officer, RAF.

DFC. No details were found.

OBE. This was gazetted on 26/9/19.

HARRISON (Francis Charles). CONWAY 1907/08. Lieutenant, RN.

DSO with BAR.

CROIX DE GUERRE: 22/6/17. He served in Coastal Motor Boats, including the Zeebrugge raid. 'Was in charge of a CMB Division operating off Ostend. Led his division with conspicuous ability and resource, and carried out the whole programme up to the last moment. Laid out the calcium flares to mark the pier ends in a most efficient manner under a heavy fire from shore batteries and machine-guns.' He survived the war.

HEADLAM (Edward James). CONWAY 1887/89. Commander RIM, (Temporary Commander, RN).

DSO: 11/1/16. He was a Naval Transport Officer in East Africa.

MiD on four occasions. One by Lieutenant-General J C Smuts, C in C East African Force, for good services, 30/1/17, and also for good services during the Rufigi River Delta operations, 19/2/18. Headlam seems to have served continually in East African operations. Incidentally, he was a hydrographic surveyor in India, 1897-1914

CGM: 31/12/18. For valuable service rendered during the War. He had been Principal Naval Transport Officer in South and East Africa.

CSI: 30/5/24. Headlam had been the Director of Royal Indian Marine in Bombay.

KNIGHTED, 29/3/29, by the Prince of Wales as His Majesty was unwell.

After a long and honourable career, Sir Edward died in 1943.

HEGARTY (Leopold Joseph). CONWAY NK. Acting Lieutenant, RNR.

MiD: 19/7/18. For distinguished services on the night of 22/23 April, 1918. This must refer to the Zeebrugge Raid. 'Throughout the operations he was of the greatest assistance, performing any duty required of him with promptness and fearlessness in an exposed position, and at times under heavy fire'. Hegarty was on board HMS DAFFODIL.

DSC. It must have been awarded subsequent to the MiD after the Zeebrugge Raid.

HOLLOWAY (Graham Charles). CONWAY NK. Commander, RD, RNR.
OBE: 1/7/19. There is a long list of awards 'in recognition of the services of the Officers of the Royal Naval Transport Service'. A number of OCs received this award.

HORDEN (Edward Joseph Calverly). CONWAY 1881/83. Captain, RIM.
CIE: 20/7/20. The search states 'Order of the Star of India for meritorious ......' but that was all.
He was the father of the actor, the late Sir Michael Hordern.

HORSBOROUGH (Gordon Stavely). CONWAY NK. Acting Commander, RD, RNR.
OBE: 1/7/19. Given under the general heading '... in recognition of services in the Royal Naval Transport Service.'

HUDDLESTON (Ernest Whiteside). CONWAY NK. Commander, RIM.
CMG: 2/6/16. For valuable services rendered in connection with the War as a Senior Marine Transport Officer in Bombay.

HUDDLESTONE (W B). CONWAY 1880/82. Commander, RIM.
MiD: 4/7/16. He was mentioned in the report by General Beauchamp Duff, C in C India, after an attack by gunfire on Madras by the German cruiser EMDEN.

HUGHES (Robert Herbert Wilfred). CONWAY NK. Brigadier.

DSO.

CMG: 25/8/17. He was a Brigadier-General and received this award for services rendered in connection with Military Operations in the Field in Mesopotamia. He was serving with the Administrative and HQ Staff and was the Director of Inland Waterways Transport.

Hughes was also listed as Commander, RNR, and Commander, RIM.

CSI: 23/4/18. For meritorious services in Mesopotamia.

CB: 9/9/21. He was a Temporary Lieutenant-Colonel and received this award for valuable services in connection with Military Operations in Mesopotamia whilst serving in the Inland Waterways Directorate.

HUGHES (Thomas). CONWAY NK. Lieutenant, RNR.

DSC: 10/8/17. For 'services in action with enemy submarines'. Hughes served in Q-Ships in European waters.

BAR to DSC: 30/10/17.

HUGHES-HALLETT (Henry Phillip). CONWAY 1905/07. Lieutenant, RIM.

DSC: 10/8/17. During operations in Mesopotamia with no specific citation. This campaign is not well regarded in history … there were many casualties and little gain.

MBE: 20/7/20. He was by this time attached to the Aden Field Force and the award was for valuable services.

Incidentally, there was also another OC Bertram Hughes-Hallett in the RIM who was probably an older brother.

HUNT (George Percy Edward). CONWAY 76/78. Lieutenant, RN.

DSO: 6/11/00. For services during the war in South Africa. Captain G P E Hunt, DSO, RN, lost his life while serving in HMS VIVID in 1917.

IRVING (Robert Beaufin). CONWAY NK. Lieutenant-Commander, RD, RNR.

OBE: 29/7/19. For valuable services as Naval Transport Officer in Charge of Landing of Naval Stores on the Palestine Coast.

Sir Robert Irving became Commodore, Cunard White Star, during WW Two.

ISAAC (Frederick Harry). CONWAY NK. Flight Sub-Lieutenant RNAS and RAF.

DFC. Several gazettes track his movements: to Temporary Flight Sub-Lieutenant, RNAS, (20/5/16) and his transfer to a Permanent Commission in RAF, 1/8/19. He was promoted from Flying Officer to Flight Lieutenant, 30/12/24. The award of the DFC must have been between 1919 and 1924.

JONES (Gerald Henry Lee). CONWAY 1906/08. Lieutenant, RNR.

DSC: 17/9/18. For services in minesweeping operations from 1st January to the 30th of June 1918.

JONES (Henry Ellington). CONWAY 1905/07. Lieutenant, Army.

MC: 5/3/18. For conspicuous gallantry and devotion to duty. 'At short notice, and without opportunity to reconnoitre, he was ordered to retake an enemy stronghold. In spite of heavy enemy machine gun fire, he re-took the position. Although his casualties were very severe, he consolidated his position and re-organised the remainder of his men. He set a magnificent example and by his good leadership and personal influence, the fighting efficiency of his company was never impaired.' Jones served in the Gloucester Regiment in France and Belgium.

JONES (John Herbert). CONWAY 1883/85. RN.
OBE.

JONES (Owen). CONWAY NK. Captain, RN.
CBE: 30/12/18. For valuable services rendered in connection with the war. Jones was attached to Trinity House.

KEELEY (Harold Percy). CONWAY 1900/02. Lieutenant-Commander, RN.
DSC: 16/5/18. There was no specific citation apart from 'services on the Mediterranean Station'. Keeley in 1920 was placed on the Retired List; in 1924 he was promoted to Lieutenant-Commander, DSC, RN, (Retd).

KENRICK (Hubert Wynn). CONWAY NK. Commander, RD, RNR.
OBE: 4/1/18. He was a Shipping Intelligence Officer in London.

KING (Henry Douglas). CONWAY 1891/93. Commodore, VD, RNVR.

DSO: 5/11/15. For Officers of the Royal Naval Division in recognition of their services in the Gallipoli Campaign.

CROIX DE GUERRE: 10/8/17. Serving in the RND in Europe.

CBE: 10/1/19. For valuable services in connection with the War. King commanded the HOWE Battalion, RND, in France. He carried the rank of Captain.

CB: 31/5/27. During the election on 21/6/29, King was re-elected to Parliament for Paddington South.

Commodore H D King, PC, CB, CBE, DSO, VD, RNVR, died (at sea off Cornwall) in 1930.

KNOWLES (Eustace Oliver). CONWAY 1908/09. Captain, Royal Engineers.

OBE: 15/11/18. For distinguished services in connection with Military Operations in Mesopotamia when attached to the Inland Waterways Transport Unit. Knowles was buried in the Basra War Cemetery.

LA TOUCHE (George Henry Stransham). CONWAY 1886/88. Commander, RIM.

OBE: 7/1/19. He served as Deputy Port Officer in Calcutta.

LABEY (George Thomas). CONWAY: NK. Captain, RE.

MC: 28.12/17. There was no specific citation. In December 1920, Temporary Captain G T Labey, MC, RE, was gazetted to retain the rank of Captain.

LALOR (William Goggan). CONWAY NK. Commander, RNR.

OBE: 1928. Gazette shows promotion to Sub-Lieutenant

in 1915. In 1932, he was promoted to Commander on the retired list.

LANG (George Holbraw (Holbrow)). CONWAY 1896/97. Commander, RN.

DSO: 5/3/18. For services in destroyers and torpedo boat flotillas during the period ending 31/12/17.

LAWSON (Noel John Cecil). CONWAY 1900/02. Rank unknown.

MBE.

LLOYD (Rowland Owen). CONWAY NK. Lieutenant, RN.

OBE: 18/4/19. For valuable services in command of the destroyer HMS MALLARD on the occasion of the torpedoing of RMS LEINSTER. He was responsible for saving many lives. LEINSTER was torpedoed by U-123 on 10/1/18 between Ireland and Anglesey.

LONG (W). CONWAY NK. Captain.

OBE: 30/3/20. He was attached to the South African Forces.

LORIARD (Cyril Harrington Grier). CONWAY NK. Second Lieutenant.

MC: 26/11/17. There was no specific citation. Gazette consists of twelve pages of awards to Army personnel of all ranks. A surprising number of Conways elected to fight in the Army in WW One. He was a Master Mariner and continued at sea after the War.

LOVEGROVE (Alfred Victor Robertson). CONWAY NK. Commander, RD, RNR.

DSO: 8/4/19. For service in the Auxiliary Patrol between 1st July and 11th November, 1918; for services in drifters, trawlers and yachts.

MacGREGOR (Ivor Gregor). CONWAY 1908/10. Lieutenant-Commander, RNR.

DSC. Gazette 14/3/19 lists Ivor G MacGregor's promotion to Lieutenant, RNR, (no DSC). Gazette of 18/6/26 shows Lieutenant-Commander I G MacGregor, DSC, RD, RNR, placed on the Retired List.

MiD. He appears again in WW Two with a MiD.

MACKAY (A H R). CONWAY 1905/07. Captain, Saskatchewan Rifles.

MC. He served in France with the 5th Battalion Canadian Infantry, Saskatchewan Rifles. Mackay was killed on Active Service 2/2/1917 and was buried in Sains-en-Gohelle War Cemetery.

MACKENZIE (Lucas Lawton). CONWAY 1905/08. Rank unknown.

MC.

MACKENZIE (K L). CONWAY NK. Acting Captain, RFC.

MC: 7/6/18. Gazette refers to Lieutenant (Acting Captain). Gazette 3/8/17 refers to Second Lieutenant, Special Reserve - Flying Officer. This suggests that he was attached to the RFC when he received the MC in 1918.

McLENNAN (Evan Stanley). CONWAY NK. Lieutenant, RNR.

DSC: 28/8/17. For services in action with enemy submarines.

MADAN (Arthur George). CONWAY 1909/11. Lieutenant, RN.

DSC: 30/7/18. In recognition of his service in submarines in enemy waters. The gazette also states that Acting Lieutenant Arthur G Madan, DSC, RNR, transferred to RN as Lieutenant, seniority 9/7/15.

MADGE (Ernest Edward). CONWAY NK. Lieutenant-Commander, RNR.

DSC: 14/3/16. It was stated that Madge performed good service during the landing on 25th April, under heavy fire, and subsequent days. He was an Officer of the East Mediterranean Squadron between the time of landing in the Gallipoli Peninsula in April 1915 and evacuation in December 1915 and January 1916. On 29/6/20 he was promoted to Lieutenant-Commander, RNR.

MARSHALL (Richard Nigel Onslow). CONWAY 1914/16. Midshipman, RNR.

DSC: 11/11/19. For distinguished service in HM CMB No.7 in the attack on Kronstadt Harbour on 18th August 1919. This boat piloted two others into the harbour through the forts, under heavy fire, and then patrolled the mouth of the harbour to cover their withdrawal. This was the action in which Gordon Steele won the VICTORIA CROSS.

MARSHALL (William). CONWAY NK. Commander, RD, RNR.

DSO: 14/7/16. Gazette states 'The officers and men serving in armed yachts, trawlers and drifters of the Auxiliary Patrol from 1/1/15 to 31/1/16 carried out their duties under extremely hazardous conditions of weather and exposure to enemy attack and mines'. They were probably minesweeping.

BAR to DSO: 28/12/17. In recognition of services in prosecution of the war. Marshall became a Captain in White Star Line in 2/7/20.

CB: 2/6/25. Marshall became Commodore Master, White Star Line in 1930.

MASSY (Lawrence Peel). CONWAY NK. Lieutenant, RNR.

DSC: 26/6/17. In recognition of his services in vessels of the Auxiliary Patrol.

MAY (Joseph Albert). CONWAY 1862/62. Merchant Navy.

OBE. He would have been in his mid to late sixties when he received this award and was probably a Ship's Master.

McDOWELL (Daniel). CONWAY 1894/96. Lieutenant-Commander, RN.

DSO: 1/1/17. In recognition of bravery and devotion to duty during minesweeping operations.

McKINSTRY (Edward Robert). CONWAY NK. Captain, RNR, (Retd).

CBE. The Gazette for the CBE was not located, but on 11/2/18 Commander McKinstry, CBE, RD, RNR (Retd) was promoted to Captain, RNR, (Retd), 'in recognition of war service'.

McLAUGHLIN (Cyril Edward). CONWAY 11/13. Acting Lieutenant, RN.

DSO (posthumous):14/10/19. This was awarded in recognition of the gallantry and devotion to duty displayed by him in sweeping and destroying mines, often under heavy enemy fire. He served in HMS HUMBER in the Davina River Flotilla. McLaughlin was killed 5/10/19 in North Russia and was buried in Archangel Cemetery.

McMICKAN (Walter Campbell). CONWAY 1885/87. Commander, RN.

OBE: 27/6/19. For valuable services at home and abroad throughout the war. The gazette of 19/9/20 shows him being placed on the Retired List as Commander.

MELLIN (Arthur Alured). CONWAY 1886/88. Commander, RN.

DSO: 29/12/16. In recognition of the skill and determination which he showed in making a successful submarine attack on an enemy light cruiser on 19th December 1916. Mellin was placed on the Retired List as Commander, 18/10/19.

MERRIMAN (Reginald Dundas). CONWAY 1903/05. Lieutenant, RIM.

DSC. For his valuable services in connection with the defence of Kut-el-Amara, Mesopotamia.

MILNE-HENDERSON (Thomas Maxwell Stuart). CONWAY 1905/07. Major, RE, Lieutenant, RIM.

OBE: 1920. He was seconded to the RE for Inland Waterways duties in Mesopotamia, where his skills as a Hydrographic Surveyor would have been valuable. Eventually, he became the Chief of Staff of the Royal Indian Navy.

MOILLET (Hubert Mainwaring Keir). CONWAY 1892/94. Captain, Temporary Major, RE.

OBE: 28/2/19. For valuable services rendered in connection with military operations in Mesopotamia, whilst attached to the Inland Waterways Directorate.

MORGAN (John Claude Verney). CONWAY 1902/07. Lieutenant, RNR.

DSC: 26/11/18. For services in action with enemy submarines.

MORGAN (Charles Eric). CONWAY 1902/04. Lieutenant, RN.

DSO. There are no details, apart from his promotion to Lieutenant, RN, 11/10/11.

MiD: 5/3/20. For valuable services in Northern European waters.

MORLAND (Henry). CONWAY 1891/93. Captain, RIM.

CIE: 31/5/21. He obviously served in India and probably received the award on retirement after thirty-six years service.

MOSSOP (Felix John). CONWAY 1915/17. Midshipman, RNR.

MiD. Mossop was twice Mentioned in Despatches. The first was for distinguished services on the night of 22/23 April,

1918. Further entry describes the incident: 'He was Second in Command of a Coastal Motor Boat during the attack made by this boat on vessels inside the mole at Zeebrugge. He displayed great coolness'. The second 'mention' was for miscellaneous services as part of the Dover Patrol.

MUIRHEAD (Malcolm). CONWAY NK. Lieutenant, RNR.
DSC: 4/6/18. The gazette is rather vague and merely states that the award is in recognition of services in vessels of the Auxiliary Patrol in Foreign waters from 1st January to 31st December 1917.

MULOCK (Evelyn Edmunds). CONWAY NK. Captain, Army.
MC. Two Gazettes detail his progress from Second Lieutenant, 13/10/14, to Temporary Captain, 10/12/15. Captain E E Mulock, MC, was seconded to the West African Frontier Force, 28/5/19, and served in the Duke of Cornwall's Light Infantry.

NANSON (Eric Roper Curzon). CONWAY 1897/99. Squadron Commander, RNAS. Group Captain, RAF.
DSO: 15/6/17. In recognition of services with the East African Military Force. 'He organised his unit with great efficiency and zeal, and carried out reconnaissance and work under great climatic difficulties'. Nanson was a Sub-Lieutenant, RNR, in 1906 and was granted a commission in RN, 17/2/14, as Lieutenant. Lloyds Captain's register shows he qualified Master 1908, Extra-Master 1908, Steamship 1908 and Steam 1909. Nanson joined the Royal Flying

Corps and reached the rank of Major, Acting Colonel.

AFC: 31/12/18. By this time Nanson was in the RNAS. Captain Geoffrey de Havilland was on the same list. Nanson was on 27/1/20 granted a Permanent Commission in the RAF. He attained the rank of Group Captain

CBE: 15/3/29. For services rendered in connection with operations against the Akhwan in the Southern Desert, Iraq, during November 27th to May 28th. On 4/7/32 he was placed on the Retired List at his own request.

NIBLETT (Henry Seawell Frank). CONWAY 1865/67. Admiral, RN.

CVO: 6/8/07. On the occasion of the inspection of His Majesty's Fleet. Niblett was Commanding Officer of the Devonport Division. Vice-Admiral H S F Niblett, CVO, RN, was promoted to Admiral, (Retired), 21/3/13.

NICHOLLS (Arthur S M). CONWAY NK. Commander, RNR.

OBE: 28/8/18. Nicholls was placed on the Retired List at own request and promoted Commander.

NICHOLSON (G) CONWAY NK. Temporary Captain, Army.

MC. There are several gazettes for G. Nicholson, 1916 to 1920, showing that the MC was probably awarded in 1917. He served in the Hampshire Regiment.

OPPEN (Hans). CONWAY NK. Lieutenant-Commander, RD, RNR.

DSO: 5/4/18. For services in vessels of the Royal Navy

employed in Patrol and Escort duties during the period 1st January to 31st December, 1918.

PAGET (John Otho). CONWAY NK. Temporary Captain, Royal Sussex Regiment.

MC: 31.5.18.

PARK (J). CONWAY NK. Rank unknown.

CBE. No details found.

PEIRSE (Richard Henry). CONWAY 1873/75. Admiral, RN.

MVO: 9/10/03. Presented on the occasion of His Majesty's visit to Austria whilst serving in HMS DIDO (Cruiser Escort) in the Home Fleet.

KCB: 19/6/14. By this time he was a Rear-Admiral.

KBE: 4/6/18. Peirse's rank was now Admiral and he was a Naval Member of the Board of Invention and Research. He retired in 1919. Note that he was the father of R E C Peirse.

PEIRSE (Richard Edmund Charles). CONWAY 1906/08. Lieutenant Colonel, RFC, (RNAS). Air Marshall, RAF.

DSO: Before May 1915. He is gazetted as 'seeing much action along the Belgian coast, attacking submarine bases' whilst serving in the RFC (Naval Wing).

AFC: 31/12/18. He served in Bomber Command.

CROCE di GUERRA (Italy): 4/4/19. For services in the Mediterranean serving in the RFC (Naval Wing). Peirse was granted a commission as Flight Lieutenant, RAF, in 1920. His career had started when he was appointed Sub-Lieutenant, RNVR, 1/11/12.

KCB: 1/6/40. Air Marshall Sir Richard Edmund Charles

Pierce was the Air Officer in Command of Bomber Command, United Kingdom. He died in 1970.

PERFECT (Herbert Mosley). CONWAY 1882/84. Captain, RN.

OBE: 31/12/18. For valuable services rendered in connection with the War.

DSM (USA): 9/12/19. Perfect now held the rank of Captain and this medal was awarded for distinguished services during the war. Permission was granted to wear the decoration.

PINCKNEY (Leonard Dunford (or Durnford)). CONWAY 1883/85. Master Mariner, Merchant Navy.

OBE. The gazette posts death notice in respect of Pinckney, having died on 23/10/1924 in the British Hospital, Port Said. He is described as Master Mariner of Salisbury.

POYNTZ (Alban Rahere Castleton). CONWAY 1902/04. Captain, RIM.

DSC: 31/3/05. No detail found. Captain A R C Poyntz, DSC, RIM, (Retd), died in 1968 in Teignmouth.

PRETTY (Francis Cecil). CONWAY 1904/07. Acting Lieutenant, RNR.

DSC: 23/3/17. There was no citation as a number of Officers were listed together. Captain F C Pretty, DSC, OBE, Master of M/V NOTTINGHAM was lost with his ship in WW Two.

PURDON (Andrew). CONWAY NK. Lieutenant, RNR.

LEGION d'HONNEUR: 23/3/17. For distinguished services rendered during the War.

RAINEY (Herbert French). CONWAY NK. Lieutenant, RNR.

DSC: 17/9/18. For services in action with enemy submarines.

RAW (Frederick Edward). CONWAY 1906/08. Lieutenant, RN.

MiD: 20/7/17. For services in action with enemy submarines.

DSC. No details found.

REDHEAD (Charles Mahon). CONWAY 1887/88. Acting Captain, RD, RNR.

DSO: 28/12/17. For services in the prosecution of the War.

RICHARDSON (Frederick Albert). CONWAY 1900/02. Lieutenant, RN.

DSC: 28/8/17. For services in action with enemy submarines. 'The Conway' contains a brief biography of Commander F A Richardson, DSC, RN, who was Captain Superintendent in CONWAY from 1927 to 1934. He transferred from the RNR to the RN in 1913 and won the DSC in Special Service ships (Q-ships).

MiD (2).

Richardson was CCC and Gold Medallist in CONWAY in 1902.

RICHARDSON (N S). CONWAY NK. Rank unknown. MM. No details found.

RICHARDSON (Sidney Sherlock). CONWAY NK. Acting Commander, RD, RNR,
OBE: 4/6/18. He was the Officer in charge of Defensive Armament at the Admiralty attached to the Trade Division.

ROBINSON (Charles Wood). CONWAY 1885? Sub-Lieutenant, RNR.
ALBERT MEDAL: 25/6/95. There is a detailed citation describing how Robinson dived over the side, fully clothed, to try and rescue a would-be suicide. The man succeeded in drowning himself and Robinson was recovered in an exhausted state. This occurred on board TEUTONIC in St. George's Channel. Robinson was the Third Officer.

ROPER (Geoffrey Stapleton Rowe). CONWAY 1905/07. Temporary Captain, Army.
MC: 25/8/16. For conspicuous gallantry in action. He led his men with great dash in the assault and afterwards crawled back to the trenches to make a report. He then returned to his platoon, being under close and heavy fire the whole time. Roper was serving in the Yorkshire Regiment on the Western Front. He was 'Killed in Action', 12/5/1917, and was buried at Cabaret-Rouge, Souchez. He had been transferred as Temporary Captain to the Liverpool Regiment on 8/5/17.

ROSTRON (Arthur Henry). CONWAY 1882/84. Captain, RD, RNR.
CONGRESSIONAL GOLD MEDAL (US) and

AMERICAN CROSS OF HONOUR: 1912. They were awarded in recognition of his work in rescuing TITANIC survivors. He was the Master of the CARPATHIA.

MiD: 1916. This was recorded for transport duties at the Dardenelles aboard HM Transport, ALAUNIA. He had MiD. The next mention in the gazette states that he had been promoted to Captain.

CBE: 31/12/18. This was awarded in recognition of valuable services rendered in connection with the War. After the War he returned to Cunard as Captain, RD, CBE, ADC, RNR.

KBE: 1926. No details found, but he was the Master of RMS MAURETANIA. Sir Arthur Rostron died in 1940.

ROWE (John Trewhella). CONWAY NK. Lieutenant, RNR.

DSC: 26/6/17. In recognition of services in vessels of the Auxiliary Patrol from the 1st February to the 31st December, 1916.

ROYDS (Charles William Rawson). CONWAY 1890/92. Admiral, RN.

ORDER OF THE RISING SUN (Third Class): 26/11/18. It was awarded by the order of the Emperor of Japan for distinguished services during the War. Japan was then Britain's ally.

CMG: 30/5/19. In recognition of service during the War. Royds had an older brother, who was also an Admiral.

KBE: 31/5/29. He was an Admiral by this time and was Deputy Commissioner of Police of the Metropolis of London. Admiral Sir Charles Royds died suddenly in office in 1931 aged 53.

ROYSE (Reverend Thomas Henry Foorde Russell). CONWAY NK. Chaplain to the Forces, Third Class, Army.

ORDER OF THE WHITE EAGLE: 13/2/17. This was conferred by Field Marshal His Imperial Majesty the Emperor of Russia.

MC: 11/10/21. The gazette notes the appointment of Royse as Honorary Chaplain to the Forces, Third Class, and quotes him as having won the Military Cross during 1918-19 in the Army Chaplain's Department.

RUDDELL (Archibald Henry L S). CONWAY 1876? Lieutenant, RN.

DSC: 29/6/17. In recognition of minesweeping operations from 1st July, 1916 to 31st March, 1917. He was promoted to Temporary Lieutenant-Commander, 25/8/17.

SCOTT (Charles Arthur). CONWAY 1895/97. Lieutenant, RIM.

DSO: 22/12/16. For services rendered in connection with Military Operations in the Field in Mesopotamia.

SCUDAMORE (John H H) CONWAY 1895? Lieutenant-Commander, RNR.

DSC. The gazette shows on 22/6/17 that Lieutenant-Commander John H H Scudamore, DSC, RNR, had been awarded the RD.

SEGRAVE (Thomas George). CONWAY 1877/79. Captain, RIM.

OBE: 4/1/18. For services in connection with the War. Segrave was Shipping Surveyor and Adviser at the India Office in London.

CBE: 26/3/20. Captain Segrave, RNR, received this honour for services in connection with the war whilst attached to the India Office in London. He had been appointed Honorary Commander, RNR, on 8/9/14.

SEROPIAN (Charles Dickran Oliver Deodat). CONWAY NK. Acting Lieutenant, RN.
OBE: 21/3/19. For devotion to duty while serving in the submarine hunting flotilla of the Northern Patrol Force.

SLADE (Frederic W P). CONWAY NK. Lieutenant, RNVR.
MC (Greece): 8/8/19. The King gave unrestricted permission to wear this Foreign Decoration. The Decoration was conferred by the King of the Hellenes.
THE ORDER OF GEORGE I, MILITARY CROSS.

SMITH (or Basden-Smith) (Henry Philip Basden). CONWAY 1895? Commander, RNR.
DSO. Several Gazettes chart his progress from Sub-Lieutenant to Lieutenant (1905), the RD in 1910, to Commander in 1918. He is shown in 1917 as having the DSO.

STAFFORD (Walter). CONWAY NK. Lieutenant, RNR.
DSC: 26/6/17. In recognition of his services in a vessel of the Auxiliary Patrol from 1st February to 31st December, 1916.

STUDD (Theodore Quintus). CONWAY 1909/11. Group Captain, RAF.
DFC: 20/9/18. As pilot he had been engaged in more

than sixty successful bombing raids many miles behind the enemy lines. Captain Studd was a most skilful pilot who could always be relied upon to carry out any task he may be called upon to perform, no matter what adversity. In 1919, he was commissioned into the RAF as Flight Lieutenant. In 1985, Group Captain Studd lived in Exmouth. It is said that Studd taught Douglas Bader to fly. He was a Gold Medallist, 1911, in CONWAY.

STURROCK (Peter Alexander Crawford). CONWAY 1904/05. Lieutenant, RN.

DSC: 29/12/16. In recognition of bravery and devotion to duty during minesweeping operations. Sturrock was lost with HMS PENARTH, which was mined and sunk off Yorkshire coast, 4/2/19.

SYMNS (Bernard Herbert). CONWAY NK. Lieutenant, RNR.

DSC: 7/8/15. In recognition of services in the Patrol Cruisers since the outbreak of War.

TAYLOR (Hastings Elwin). CONWAY 1893/96. Lieutenant-Commander, RNVR.

OBE: 9/8/19. For valuable services as a Military Control Officer in Spain during the War.

THOMPSON (William Peter). CONWAY 1869/70. Lieutenant-Commander, RNR.

OBE: 4/6/18. Thompson was Marine Superintendent, Elder Dempster Shipping Co. If CONWAY dates are correct: he must have been 64 years of age and due to retire.

TURBETT (Lionel William Richard Tufnell). CONWAY 1900/02. Commodore, RIM.

OBE: 1919. For distinguished and gallant service, and devotion to duty during the Mesopotamia campaign. Turbett achieved high rank (Commodore) in the Royal Indian Navy, retiring in January 1938.

UNWIN (Edward). CONWAY 1877/79. Captain, RN.

MiD: 14/3/16. For services with the Eastern Mediterranean Squadron covering the period of the evacuation of the Gallipoli Peninsula in December 1915 to January 1916.

CMG. In recognition of services with the Eastern Mediterranean Squadron covering the period of the evacuation of the Gallipoli Peninsula in December 1915 to January 1916.

VICTORIA CROSS: 13/8/18. This was awarded for his conspicuous acts of bravery. The gazette contained the official report by Vice-Admiral John de Robeck on the operation, including a fine description of Unwin's acts of personal bravery without regard to the dangers. His unit was in charge of landings at V Beach.

ORDER OF THE NILE, (Egypt): 14/3/19. No specific citation given and HM the King gave unrestricted permission for the recipient to wear.

CB. Captain Unwin, VC, CMG, RN. References after 1920 show Unwin as being the holder of the CB. In 1929 he was appointed Deputy Lieutenant for the County of Stafford.

VINCENT (Frederick Walker). CONWAY 1892/94.

OBE. No details found.

WARDEN (Arthur Richard Shaw). CONWAY 1882/84. Lieutenant-Commander, RN.
ALBERT MEDAL: 14/4/16. On 26/10/15 Warden, personally and at great personal danger, extinguished a fire in the hold of an ammunition ship. The citation concludes 'There is little doubt that the prompt and gallant action of Warden figures in CONWAY's List of Notables. He was attached to the Naval Transport Officer's Office in Boulogne.

WARDEN (St Ledger Stanley). CONWAY 1878/78. Temporary Commander, RN, Commander, RIM.
DSO: 13/3/18. For service with the Royal Naval Transport Service in France.

WARNER (Wilfred E). CONWAY 1911/13. Lieutenant, RN.
DSC. No details found.

WARREN (William Henry Farrington). CONWAY 1892/92. Commander, RAN.
DSO: 14/5/18. For services on the Mediterranean Station. Warren commanded the Australian Destroyer Flotilla operating out of Brindisi in 1918. He had been in PARRAMATA since outbreak of the War and brought the Flotilla to the Mediterranean from Australia. Warren was drowned in Brindisi Harbour while on Active Service and was buried in Brindisi, 13/4/18.

WATT (Duncan Alexander MacKinnon). CONWAY 1902/04. Lieutenant, RNR.
DSC: 17/9/18. For services in the Auxiliary Patrol,

minesweeping, and Coastal Motor Boats from 1ˢᵗ January to 30ᵗʰ June 1918.

WEBB (C P). CONWAY 1896/98. Second Lieutenant, Army.

MC. Webb served with the Queen's Own Royal West Kent Regiment, Third Battalion.

WESTGARTH (William Armstrong). CONWAY NK. Lieutenant, RNR.

DSC: 16/4/18. In recognition of his services in minesweeping operations from 1ˢᵗ April to 31ˢᵗ December 1917.

ORDER OF THE TOWER AND SWORD (Portugal): 16/4/18. It was granted by order of the President of the Portuguese Republic.

WILLIAMS (Leslie Barnard). CONWAY 1908/12. Temporary Lieutenant, RFC.

MC: 23/4/18. For conspicuous gallantry and devotion to duty. A long citation, concluded: '... his machine crashed to the earth in the open. Being wounded, he lay there unable to move, but was eventually rescued. This Officer has always shown himself to be full of zeal, determination and courage.'

WILSON (Graham Francis Winstanley). CONWAY 1902/03. Commander, RN.

DSO. The gazette of 2/7/20 published his promotion to Commander and mentions DSO.

WILSON (Roger Parker). CONWAY 1884/86. Lieutenant-Colonel, Indian Medical Service.

CIE: 2/6/25. This was awarded to the Officiating Surgeon-General to the Government of Bengal.

WRIGHT (Allan G). CONWAY NK. Army.

CBE. An Allan G Wright is listed in the Leicester Regiment, 1915-1918.

YARDLEY (Archibald Talbot). CONWAY NK. Lieutenant, RNR.

DSC: 19/9/18. For services in vessels employed in Escort, Convoy and Patrol duties from 1st January to 30th June 1918.

CONWAY HEROES

CHAPTER FIVE

CADET SCHOOL SHIP HMS CONWAY
WORLD WAR TWO HONOURS

 HMS CONWAY HONOURS WWII

ADAMS (Alwyn William Reginald). CONWAY 1928/30. Lieutenant-Commander, RN.
DSC: 24/11/44. For gallantry, skill, determination and undaunted devotion to duty during the landing of Allied Forces on the coast of Normandy. Adams commanded ORESTES, a minesweeper, from 22/10/43 to 16/10/44.

AITKEN (John Gordon). CONWAY NK. Temporary Lieutenant, RNR.
MiD: 28/7/42. For good services when a merchantman was set on fire in Tobruk harbour. Aitken was the Commanding Officer of POLYANTHUS when she sunk U-952, with the loss of all hands, 21/9/43.

ALINGTON (Patrick Hamilton). CONWAY NK. Wing Commander, RAF.
DFC: 11/8/41. A long citation extolled his outstanding ability and leadership in command first of a Sunderland aircraft and then of the Squadron. He carried out some

177

remarkable work during the evacuation from Greece to Crete when attached to No. 230 Squadron in the Mediterranean.

MiD: 28/12/45. He retired as Wing Commander on 23rd June 1963.

ALINGTON (William James). CONWAY NK. Acting Wing Commander, RAF.

DFC: 29/1/43. Has completed a large number of sorties and has destroyed two enemy aircraft at night. Extremely able flight commander whose success in night fighting has been most praiseworthy. No. 25 Squadron.

BAR to DFC: 20/7/43. Displayed exceptional keenness and determination to inflict loss upon the enemy ... 7 locomotives; 4 aircraft on the ground and a hangar; a minesweeper. He displays fearless and skilful leadership. No. 264 Squadron. Action over Europe.

AFC. Probably awarded towards end of career when he was an Acting Wing Commander.

ALLAN (George). CONWAY 1928/30. Lieutenant-Commander, RNR.

MiD: 12/11/40. For good services in HM Submarines in recent patrols and operations against the enemy.

RD: 26/7/46.

ALLEN (Robert Swinton). CONWAY 1929/31. Wing Commnander, RAF.

DFC: 25/6/40. During darkness, sighted a Heinkel 111 and manoeuvred his aircraft to enable his Sergeant WOP/AG to shoot it down; then chased a Ju 87 which crashed and burned, before continuing to target. His initiative, outstanding skill and resolution contributed to the success of many operations. No. 49 Squadron operating over Europe. He was probably flying a Hampden, based at Coningsby, Lincs. Allen had joined RAF in 1935. Possibly he was one of several OCs who moved to the RAF when jobs were scarce at sea in the 1930s.

BAR to DFC: 24/12/40.

DSO: 2/9/41. Raids on German warships in Brest, La Pelice and Cherbourg: bravery, determination and resource displayed by the leader and air crews. No 106 Squadron in Bomber Command. The Hampden was succeeded by the Manchester and then the Lancaster. Wing Commander R S Allen, DSO, DFC*, RAF, retired at own request, 2//3/56.

ALLINGTON (William James). Conway NK. Flight Lieutenant, RAF.

AFC: 26/9/41. There is no specific citation. He was promoted from Sergeant Pilot to Pilot Officer in April 1936.

ANCHOR (Herbert John). CONWAY 1910/12. Commodore, RD, RNR.

OBE: 1/1/42. Anchor was based in HMS EAGLET, Liverpool.

MiD: 5/6/45 for 3 years service as Commodore Ocean Convoys.

ANDERSON (Alan Hamilton Barnett). CONWAY NK. Lieutenant, RNR.

DSC: 3/10/41. For courage, skill and enterprise in successful submarine patrols serving in HM S/M RORQUAL. Anderson seems to have spent the whole war in submarines.

He was in command of SCOTSMAN, 15/8/44 until end of War.

ANDREW (Bruce John Bevis). CONWAY 1934/36. Commander, RN.

DSC: 28/4/42. For bravery and skill in successful submarine operations in HM S/M THUNDERBOLT (ex-THETIS) in the Atlantic and Mediterranean.

MiD: 24/9/43. For outstanding bravery, skill and devotion to duty in successful patrols in HM Submarines. He was Commanding Officer of HM S/M UNUBROKEN in the Mediterranean.

OBE. No details found.

Andrew married Rosemary Goddard, the daughter of the Commanding Officer of CONWAY. Commander Andrew, DSC, OBE, RN retired 1969 and died December 1985. He was well known as 'The wing-collar man' because he favoured wing collars!

ANTHES (Denis del Strother). CONWAY NK. Chief Officer, Merchant Navy.

MBE: 28/4/44. In convoys under continual threat from enemy submarines … exceptional courage, skill and his efficiency and leadership played an important part in the dangerous and vital operations, (Battle of the Atlantic).

APLIN (Charles Peter D'Auvergne). CONWAY NK. Lieutenant, RNR.

MiD: 23/3/45. For distinguished service and gallantry during the invasion of the South of France.

ATKINS (Maurice Dudley). CONWAY 39/41. Second Officer, Merchant Navy.

MBE: 6/1/45. For his actions during the loss of the EMPRESS OF ASIA in 1942, and EMPRESS OF CANADA. Canadian Pacific Steamship.

BAILEY (George). CONWAY 1930/31. Acting Commander, RIM.

DSC: 28/6/46. Awarded for distinguished services in the Far East.

BAKER (aka Croft-Baker), (Alan Jack Croft), CONWAY 1937/39. Acting Sub-Lieutenant, RNR.

MiD: 15/11/42. For bravery and devotion to duty (Posthumous). Killed on board HMS KIPLING in the Eastern Mediterranean.

BALL (Granville Murray). CONWAY NK. Lieutenant,

MiD: 19/11/43. For courage and endurance in defence against enemy air attack while on Convoy Escort Duty in HMS SHOREHAM.

BALL (Kenneth Rhodes). CONWAY 1933/35. Flight Lieutenant, RAF.

MiD: 23/9/41. Killed in Action over Germany with No. 9 Squadron (Wellington bombers) in August 1941, and was buried near Hamburg.

BAND (Brian Hugh). CONWAY 1930/32. Lieutenant, RN.

DSC: 12/12/41. For courage, skill and resolution in successful submarine patrols in HM S/M UPHOLDER.

Band was lost in HM S/M OLYMPUS, 8/8/42, mined near Malta. There were nine survivors who swam seven miles to the island.

BARNETT (Avon Alexander). CONWAY NK. Commander, RD, RNR.
DSC: 24/1/44. For gallantry, leadership and undaunted devotion to duty under continuous fire from the enemy during landings on the Italian mainland. Barnett was the Commanding Officer of the Boarding Vessel CAMITO (ex-Elder Fyffe), 1940-41. CAMITO was sunk by a U-boat, 6/5/41.

BEARDMORE (Harold). CONWAY NK. Chaplain, AKC, RN.
OBE: 1/7/41. Beardmore was based in the UK.

BEAVER (George Duncan). CONWAY 1906/08. Major, (formerly Indian Army).
MiD: 30/4/47. Gazette states: 'reverts to unemployment on account of disability, with honorary rank of Major'.

BEDDOE (Charles Foyle). CONWAY NK. Lieutenant, RNR.
MiD: 28/7/44. '... outstanding courage, leadership, resource and determination during the assault on Anzio ... unbroken flow of supplies ... despite bombing, mining and bombardment from shore batteries.'

BELL (Charles Leigh de Hauteville). CONWAY 1916/18. Commander, RD, RNR.

DSC: 28/4/44. For courage, resolution and skill in HM Ships in successful operations with enemy submarines. He commanded various escort destroyers and ended the war in HMS PALOMARES (FD Ship). Credited with sinking U-306 on 31/10/43, NE of Azores, in command of HMS WHITEHALL (V&W Escort Destroyer) in the North Atlantic. In 1957 is reported as Master of the EMPRESS of ENGLAND.

BERNA (Salvator Peter). CONWAY 1932/34. Chief Officer, Merchant Navy.
MBE: 8/6/45. For continuous service at sea, including being torpedoed in SS BEAVERDALE in April 1941, (Third Officer).

BICKFORD (Jack Grant). CONWAY 1910/13. Captain, RN.
DSC: 22/12/39. For successful actions against enemy submarines in command of HMS EXPRESS in home waters. `DSO: 16/8/40. For good services in the withdrawal of the Allied Armies from the beaches at Dunkirk. Captain Bickford was lost in HMS EXPRESS, June 1940, during a minelaying operation off the Dutch coast.

BLAMPIED (Richard). CONWAY NK. Temporary Acting Lieutenant-Commander, RNZNR.
MBE: 28/12/45. No details found.

BOYLE (Douglas Seaman). CONWAY 1939/41. Sub-Lieutenant, RCN.
MiD. Outstanding leadership, skill and devotion to

duty in HMCS CHAUDINERE (a River Class Frigate) in a successful operation against a U-Boat (U-744 sunk in Atlantic in March 1944). Vice Admiral D S Boyle, CF, RCN, retired in 1977, and died 2001.

BLOYE (Norman Herbert Barton). CONWAY 1919/21. Lieutenant-Commander, RD, RNR.
`DSC: 23/1/45. For courage and skill in hazardous minesweeping operations off the Adriatic Coast in HMS FABIUS (Mine Sweeper/Base Adriatic).

BRAND (Eric Sydney). CONWAY 1909/10. Captain, RCN.
OBE: 2/6/43. Contributed materially to the establishment of an efficient U.S. Navy organisation for the control of shipping in co-operation with Canadian Forces. Brand was in 1942 on loan to RCN. He was attached to the Naval HQ Ottowa, (Director of Trade & Intelligence). The list in 1985 shows Captain E S Brand, OBE, RN, (Retd) in Canada. He died in 1991.

BRIGGS (William Edward Slade). CONWAY 1921/23. Captain, RCNR.
DSC: 30/6/42. For bravery, resource and devotion to duty. Canadian recommendation describes how ORILLIA took fuel from a torpedoed tanker, TACHEZ, which aided her subsequent salvage. Briggs was promoted Captain RCNR on 30/6/57.

BROOKE-ALDER (Geoffrey). CONWAY 1936/38. Acting Sub-Lieutenant, RNR.
DSC: 3/9/40. For bravery, skill and enterprise in

minesweeping operations off the coasts of Holland, Belgium and France.

BROOKES (John Geoffrey). CONWAY NK. Lieutenant, RN.

DSC: 23/4/42. For courage, endurance and devotion to duty while minesweeping in HM SPEEDY (Halcyon M/S) in Northern waters and Mediterranean.

MBE. 1959.

BROOKE-SMITH (Francis Haffey). CONWAY 1934/36. Sub-Lieutenant, RNR.

GEORGE CROSS: 24/6/41. For great gallantry and undaunted devotion to duty. Mine disposal on the Manchester Ship Canal. Member of a Conway 'dynasty'.

BROWN (Patrick Richards). CONWAY 1921/22. Acting Lieutenant-Commander, RD, RNR.

MiD: 25/7/44. After the assault on Anzio, 'despite bombing, mining and bombardment from shore batteries'.

BURKE (Wick Bernard). CONWAY 1908/09.

KBE. Burke is listed as a 'Retired Officer' re-employed in two Gazettes 1940 and 1947. Captain, (Major). No further details.

BUXTON (Sydney William). CONWAY 1929/32. Temporary Lieutenant, RCNVR.

MiD: 8/6/44. Displayed courage and devotion to duty in that he re-entered a burning tanker hatch in order to assist in the rescue of two Naval firefighters in HMCS VERLAINE.

CAMBRIDGE (John Stephen). CONWAY 1917/19. Temporary Acting Lieutenant-Commander, RNVR.

DSC: 10/11/42. For bravery in action against the enemy while serving in HM Gun Boats with the East Coast Coastal Forces.

CAMERON (John). CONWAY 1904/06. Captain, RIN.

CIE: 28/12/43. Cameron was the Principal Officer, Mercantile Marine Department, in Calcutta for thirty-seven years. He entered the Royal Indian Marine in 1906.

CAMPBELL (John Duncan). CONWAY 1902/04. Colonel, Indian Army.

DSO. This was awarded in First World War probably in India.

DSC: 21/3/19. For services in minesweeping from 1st July to 31st December, 1918.

OBE: 2/6/39. Stated 'retired on an Indian Pension, 3/4/39. Gazette 9/6/44 stated 'ceased to belong to the Indian Reserve of Regular Officers.'

CANN (Denis More). CONWAY 1909/11. Lieutenant-Commander, RN.

DSC:24/9/40. For services in Norway HM A/S Trawler INDIAN STAR escorting an East Coast Convoy.

CARROLL (Charles Laurence). CONWAY 1923/25. Acting Lieutenant-Commander, RNR.

DSC: 29/12/42. Outstanding service in the face of the enemy ... zeal, patience, cheerfulness and for setting an example, without which the high tradition of the Royal Navy could not have been upheld. Carroll was the Commanding Officer of HM M/S Trawler NOBLE NORA in the Mediterranean.

CASEY (Denis Arthur). CONWAY 1902/04. Commodore, RD, RNR.
DSC: 24/10/16. Awarded for service in submarines in WW One.
CBE: 1942. Awarded before the DSO, when he was a Commodore of Convoys in the Atlantic and Northern waters. Casey was Master of Royal Mail ANDES, 1948/49 and ADC to the King, 1944.
DSO: 21/7/42. For bravery, seamanship and resolution in bringing a convoy from Murmansk in the face of relentless and determined attacks by enemy U-boats and aircraft.

CHARD (Edward Rex) CONWAY NK. Sub-Lieutenant, RNVR.
MiD: 2/6/44.

CHODZKO (Michael Anthony). CONWAY 1925/28. Sub-Lieutenant, RNVR.
MiD (1): 16/8/40. For good services in the withdrawal of Allied Armies from the beaches at Dunkirk in Motor Boat AURA.
MiD (2). Details not found.

CHRISTIAN (John Macindoe). CONWAY 1928/30. Lieutenant, RN.
MiD: 25/6/40. For daring and resource in the conduct of hazardous and successful operations by the Fleet Air Arm on the Coast of Norway, serving in ARK ROYAL.

DSC. No record found, but DSC was post-June 1940.

CLARKE (Richard Thomas). CONWAY NK. Third Officer, Merchant Navy.

MBE: 29/1/43. After the ship was torpedoed and sunk, one of the boats made a voyage of twenty days before being picked up. It was due to the courage, skill and fortitude of Mr. Clarke during the latter part of the voyage that the boat was brought to safety. Ten of the occupants died.

CLARKE (Winston Raymond). CONWAY 1915/16. Rank unknown.

DSC. No details.

MiD. No details.

CLIBBORN (William Lancelot). CONWAY NK. Captain, Merchant Navy.

OBE: 28/5/43. No details.

CLUTTERBUCK (David G. C.). CONWAY 1926/29. Vice-Admiral, RN.

KBE

CB

Deputy Supreme Allied Commander Atlantic.

Details under Conway Notables.

COLLINSON (Frank Bentley). CONWAY NK. Lieutenant-Commander, RNR.

MiD: 9/6/40. For successful submarine patrols in HM S/M TETRACH.

MiD: 25/6/42. Murmansk convoys, 3/5/42, in HMS

OXSLIP, (Flower Class), in North Atlantic. Commanded three escort vessels from August 1940-1945.

DSC: 30/11/43. U-436 sunk in North Atlantic West of Cape Ortega, Spain, 26/5/43, by HMS TEST, (River Class Frigate).

COOMBS (William Harry). CONWAY 1907/09. Captain, Merchant Navy, Honorary Commander, RNR.

CBE: 6/6/47. Captain Coombs was the pioneer of improvement for conditions of employment for Officers of the Merchant Navy and was much involved with the MMSA and management of CONWAY. He was President of the Officers Merchant Navy Federation, Ltd. A man of small stature but large heart (compiler's opinion).

COOPER (Jack Winston). CONWAY 1924/26. Acting Lieutenant-Commander, RNR.

DSC: 19/9/44. Sinking of U-765 on 6/5/44. For courage, resolution and skill in anti-U-Boat operations in HMS BLIGH (Captain Class Frigate) in the Atlantic.

BAR to DSC: 11/9/45. Sinking of U-636 in North Atlantic, West of Ireland, 21/4/45 in HMS BAZELY (Captain Class Frigate).

CORKHILL (Anthony David). CONWAY 1934/38. Midshipman (A), RN.

DSC: 19/7/40. For gallantry and coolness in action against heavy odds off the coast of Norway whilst serving in HMS DEVONSHIRE, (Heavy Cruiser). Commander A D Corkhill, DSC, lives in Salcombe and is an active member of Conway Club.

COUGHLAN (Denis Harold George). CONWAY 1925/27. Lieutenant, RNR.

MiD: 17/12/43. For gallant and distinguished services and untiring devotion to duty in operations which led to the capture of Sicily (Operation Husky) whilst serving in HMS BOSTON, (Minesweeper).

DSC: 5/5/44. For great skill, endurance and devotion to duty in clearing enemy minefields to enable supply convoys and bombardment forces to operate in support of the 8th Army in their advance from Egypt to Tunisia. Lieutenant-Commander Coughlan was serving in HMS CROMARTY, (Minesweeper).

Captain D H G Coughlan, DSC, RD** RNR was awarded a 3rd clasp to the RD 22/4/66, and died in 1989.

COULTAS (Ernest). CONWAY NK. Captain, Merchant Navy.

OBE: 19/3/40. Won an encounter with a U-Boat: ' ... by resolute handling of his ship, by brilliantly forestalling the enemy's movements and courageously holding his course and speed ... he saved his ship.' He also forced the submarine to dive, leaving its gun crew in the sea, who were then saved. He was Master of the CLAN MACBEAN and the action took place in the Atlantic.

CRABB (Lionel Kenneth). CONWAY 1922/24. Commander, RNVR.

GEORGE MEDAL: 21/1/44. For gallantry and undaunted devotion to duty. Clearance Diver in Mediterranean. Details in GM chapter.

OBE: 7/12/45. For distinguished service in the War in Europe.

He is the famous 'Buster' Crabb.

CRICK (Trevor George Payne). CONWAY 1915/17. Commander, RN.

DSC. Commanded HMS HUSSAR, a minesweeper, at outbreak of war. Nothing found re this award ... may have been WW1.

BAR to DSC: 10/9/43. For great skill and daring in action with enemy submarines in the Atlantic. Sank Italian S/M LEONARDO do VINCI, NE from the Azores. By this time Crick was Acting Commander and commanded HMS NESS (River Class Frigate).

MiD: 22/12/44. He was commanding HMS JASON and the citation must have been the same time as he won the OBE. They were involved with the Normandy Landings.

OBE: 1/12/44. For great courage and skill under attack from the air. Crick was the Senior Officer of the group of minesweepers that came under attack from RAF Typhoon fighters off Le Havre 27/8/44 ... HMS BRITOMART and HUSSAR. SALAMANDER damaged and they suffered casualties in JASON. This was an appalling 'friendly fire' case, which was blamed on Foreign Office British Assault Area's intelligence. In an interview in 1969, Commander Crick said, "It was a queer way to get a gong".

CROCKETT (John Alexander). CONWAY 1931/33. Temporary Lieutenant, RNR.

MiD: 29/12/44. No specified citation.

CROZIER (Robert Arthur). CONWAY NK. Lieutenant-Commander, RD, RNR.

MiD: 10/11/44. For gallantry, skill and devotion to duty during the landing of Allied Forces on the coast of Normandy.

DAY (Archibald). CONWAY 1913/14. Vice-Admiral, RN.
DSO: 1/5/45. For courage, efficiency and devotion to duty in establishing navigation aids in the Approaches to the Rangoon River, in minesweeping and the survey of the river prior to the assault on the city in May 1945. He was in HM Surveying Ship WHITE BEAR.
CB. No record, but served on the staff of Commodore, Dover 1939-1943.
Vice-Admiral Sir Archibald Day, KBE, CB, DSO, Hydrographer.

DIBLEY (George). CONWAY NK. Lieutenant-Commander, RNR.
MiD. For operations in the Shetlands in HMS PANGBOURNE.
DSC: 3/12/43. For steadfast courage and skill in dangerous and important minesweeping operations, Operation Antidote, involved the 12th Flotilla sweeping from Galita, Algeria to Susse, Tunisia in 1943.

DICKENSON (John Edward). CONWAY 1930/32. Rank unknown.
DFC. Nothing found.

DOBSON (Joseph Everard). CONWAY NK. Acting Commander, RD, RNR.
DSC: 23/2/45. Listed as awarded the RD, but does not mention DSC. Commander J P Dobson was awarded the DSC 9/7/40, possible misidentification.

DODDS (Bernard Cyril). CONWAY NK. Captain, Merchant Navy.

OBE: 22/9/44. His ship was torpedoed and sunk immediately. The Captain displayed courage, coolness and leadership of a high order. He took charge of one of the boats and brought it safely to land after fourteen days. The ship was sailing independently.

DOUGLAS (Alexander Thomas). CONWAY 1920/22. Lieutenant-Commander, RNR.

OBE: 5/5/44. For distinguished services in salvage and repair work which enabled the Port of Naples to be used by Allied shipping.

US MEDAL of FREEDOM and BRONZE STAR. The President of USA awarded Douglas this medal and permission was granted to wear it.

DOUGLAS-WATSON (Francis). CONWAY 1909/10. Acting Commander, RN.

DSO: 25/10/40. For good services in the withdrawal of the Allied Armies from the French coast on Wednesday, 29th May. Minesweeper PANGBOURNE damaged by German bombing at Dunkirk, two Officers wounded. He was killed at Piraeus when CLAN FRASER's cargo of TNT exploded and wrecked the harbour.

DOWDING (John Charles Keith). CONWAY 1904/06. Commander, RD, RNR.

DSO: 16/8/40. For good services during the withdrawal of the Allied Armies from the beaches of Dunkirk. He commanded HMS MONA'S ISLE (Armed Boarding Vessel).

Dowding served in Orient Line from 1919 and was made Staff Commander 1936.

CBE: 9/10/42. For bravery and resolution as Commodore of a North Russian Convoy. Much has been written about the fate of PQ17, which was disastrous. RIVER AFTON was sunk and survivors were picked up by HMS LOTUS. Dowding went on to participate in major WW Two events.

ADC: 9/45. Appointed by the King.

DREW (Harold). CONWAY 1909/10. Captain, RN.

DSC. Shown on WW One Honours as awarded 11/5/17. No details.

CBE: 28/12/45. Chief Staff Officer, 18th Cruiser Squadron (HMS MANCHESTER) between June 1941 and August 1942.

DREW (Thomas Bernard). CONWAY 1902/03. Vice-Admiral, RN.

OBE: 15/7/19. During chase of GOEBEN and BRESLAU by HMS GLOUCESTER.

CB: 31/12/43. Minelayers, 24/2/42 to 4/2/43 (Northern Barrage) in HMS SOUTHERN PRINCE.

DRINKWATER (J.). CONWAY 1906/07. Commander, RN.

OBE. Nothing found.

DUFF (Douglas Valder). CONWAY 1914/15. Temporary Lieutenant, RNVR.

MiD(3). Enterprise and seamanship while serving off the Libyan coast. Only one MiD found in the Gazette and

Unit histories. An adventurous character and prolific author. Commanding Officer of HM Yacht ESKIMO NELL as part of the Western Desert Schooner Flotilla, Mediterranean. His final wartime job was with the Admiralty 'Irregular Warfare Depart' in Teignmouth.

DUNCAN (John). CONWAY NK. Captain, Merchant Navy.
OBE: 27/8/43. A long citation, including: ... courage, skill and outstanding seamanship in difficult and dangerous circumstances ... valuable services to military authorities, troops and refugees ... the ship was at Singapore as the Japanese advanced. The Chief Engineer was included in this citation.

EASTON (Alan Herbert). CONWAY 1917/19. Lieutenant-Commander, RCNR.
DSC: 31/7/42. Distinguished service before the enemy. Working with two other vessels, sank U-588 on 31/7/42. He was to command two corvettes and a destroyer. At the time of this award he was in command of HMCS SACKVILLE (Flower Class) in the North Atlantic.
MiD: 3/10/44. Outstanding skill and devotion to duty in a successful action against enemy trawlers and U-boats, commanding HMCS SASKATCHEWAN.

ELLIOT (Gerald Otho Rooskie). CONWAY 1888/89. Commander, RN.
OBE. No details.

ELLIS (Robert Wilson). CONWAY 1918/20. Temporary Lieutenant. RNR.

DSC: 28/5/43. For gallantry and outstanding service, zeal, patience and cheerfulness, and for setting an example of wholehearted devotion to duty without which the high standard of the Royal Navy could not have been upheld.

ENGLISH (Malcolm Christopher). CONWAY 1929/31. Lieutenant-Commander, RNR.

MiD. He commanded KLO, a Norwegian A/S whaler and GLOXINIA (Flower Class) … in the Atlantic and Mediterranean.

ESSON (Alan Flockhart). CONWAY 1935. Lieutenant, RNR.

MiD: 27/8/40. Good services in operations off the Dutch, Belgian and French coasts. VENOMOUS, (a V and W Destroyer), was active in the evacuation of Allied forces from Europe. She continued in the role of convoy escort throughout the war.

MiD: 15/6/45. For gallantry, tenacity and undaunted devotion to duty on patrols in the Aegean area during one of the most dangerous periods of the war in the Mediterranean in command of HMS S/M ULTIMATUM.

EUMAN (Charles). CONWAY 1899/1901. Commander, RN.

MiD: 18/8/40. For services in the withdrawal of Allied Armies from the beaches at Dunkirk commanding HM SKOOT BRANDARIS, (a Balloon Vessel).

EVERETT (Douglas Henry). CONWAY 1913/14. Rear-Admiral, RN.

DSO: 23/2/40. In recognition of the gallant and successful action with the ADMIRAL GRAF SPEE. Having done as much as they could during the long months of waiting, they stood the test of battle. He served in HMS AJAX in the Battle of the River Plate.

MiD: 21/12/43. For Operation Shingle where he was Staff Officer of Force V in the invasion of Sicily

CBE. Awarded at the end of the war in the Far East where he commanded the Carrier HMS ARBITER. Everett seems to have received an MBE and also a Chilean Order of Merit. Rear-Admiral D H Everett, CB, CBE, DSO, RN died 26/8/86.

FANNING (Michael Roger Eaton)   CONWAY 1924/25. Commander, RN.

DSC: 8/1/42. States 'withdrawal from Crete' ... no further details. RM Mobile Naval Base Defence in Crete.

OBE: 1958. List 1985 shows Commander M.R.E. Faning, OBE, DSC, RN, died in 1991.

FITZMAURICE (William Vere). CONWAY NK. Sub-Lieutenant, RNR.

DSC: 8/8/41. For courage and devotion to duty during operations in the Mediterranean. Fitzmaurice and 8 ratings wounded when trawler OUSE was sunk by a mine at Tobruck.

FLETCHER (William Edmund).   CONWAY 1919/21. Lieutenant-Commander, RN.

ALBERT MEDAL (Posthumous): 13/5/41. A sad and noted event. Fletcher lost his life attempting to rescue Amy Johnson in the Thames estuary. He was the Commanding Officer of HMS HASLEMERE. ALBERT MEDAL would have become a George Cross had Fletcher survived.

FRANCOMB (Charles Edward Newall). CONWAY 1918/20. Commander, RNR.

OBE. Nothing found but he was well-known post-war as Marine Superintendent of Ocean Weather Ships (Meteorological Office).

FRASER (Ian Edward). CONWAY 1936/38. Lieutenant-Commander, RNR.

DSC: 6/4/43. Bravery in successful submarine patrols. S/M SAHIB is recorded as sinking U-301 on 21/1/43 in the Mediterranean.

VICTORIA CROSS: 9/11/45. A long citation detailing the exploit when XE.3 sank a Japanese cruiser in the Johore Strait. It includes ... courage and determination are beyond praise. Based in HMS BONA VENTURE for HM S/M XE.3. One of WW Two's most famous daring and gallant exploits.

Personal account in his book 'Frogman VC', 1957.

LEGION of MERIT (USA): 29/11/46. Awarded for outstanding services when in command of HM S/M XE-3. Fraser went on to become a pioneer in the commercial diving industry.

Lieutenant-Commander I E Fraser, VC, DSC, RD*, RNR (retd) was a Patron of the Conway Club and died in 2008.

FRASER (James Lovat). CONWAY 1933/35. Temporary Lieutenant, RNVR.

MiD (Posthumous): 18/6/43. Bravery and skill in a successful attack on enemy shipping while serving in Light Coastal Forces serving in HM MTB 233 in home waters. Buried in Killearn Parish Churchyard.

FRASER-SMITH (James Buchanan). CONWAY 1937/39. Rank unknown.

MiD. Nothing found.

GELLING (William Emerson). CONWAY NK. Lieutenant, RD, RNR.

DSC. All that was found was that on 14/6/40 awarded RD as Commanding Officer of TEROMA (Trawler M/S) and ARISTOCRAT, 1/1/41, (AA Escort Paddler).

GIBSON (William). CONWAY 1902/04. Lieutenant-Colonel, Army.

MC: 25/8/16. For conspicuous gallantry during the capture of an enemy position in France. Though wounded, he carried up a machine gun to an important position. He was serving in the Staffordshire Regiment.

DSO: 29/11/18. There is a long citation, including: 'For conspicuous gallantry and initiative when in command of his Battalion during five days operations ... reorganised ... great skills ... pursued retreating enemy … captured many important positions. His coolness and determination inspired his men and contributed to the success of the operation.' Gibson was serving in the 10th West Yorkshire Regiment.

OBE: 28/5/43. Home Guard in Buckinghamshire.

GILES (Herbert Joseph). CONWAY NK. Captain, RD, RNR, Merchant Navy.

OBE: 5/6/42. Master.

GOODWIN (George Archibald Wycliffe). CONWAY 1931/33. Lieutenant (A), RN.

OBE: 27/4/45. Nothing found. HMS GARUDA, RN Air Station, South, India. Killed 16/11/44 aged 34.

GOODWIN (Richard John Grove). CONWAY 1920s? Lieutenant-Commander, RNR.

MiD: 1/7/41. HMS BORDE described as a magnetic mine experimental craft.

DSC: 5/5/44. Minesweeping in support of Western Desert. Skill, endurance and devotion to duty in clearing enemy minefields to enable supply convoys and bombardment forces to operate in support of the 8th Army in their advance from Egypt to Tunis. Based in HMS GULLANE off the North African Coast. Lieutenant-Commander R J G Goodwin, RD, DSC, RNR retired 1/7/50.

GOWAN (Henry Carty). CONWAY 1929/30. Commander, RN.

MiD: 3/7/42. For promptness and resource in the salvage of his ship. Commander H C Gowan, OBE, RN, retired 1985.

GRAY (Henry Lord). CONWAY NK. Final rank unkmnown. RAF.

DSO. No details. Harold Lord Gray was commissioned as Pilot Officer in January 1943.

GREEN (William Victor Spiers). CONWAY 1940/43. Midshipman, RNR.

MiD: 3/3/44. For gallantry, distinguished service and devotion to duty during the action in which SCHARNHORST was engaged and sunk. Probably in HMS SHEFFIELD in Northern Arctic waters. Reported to have maintained discipline in the TS during the action.

GRIEVE (Kenneth Campbell). CONWAY 1925/28. Lieutenant, RN.

MiD: 16/5/41. For courage, enterprise, and devotion to duty in contact with the enemy and also for outstanding courage and skill in a brilliant and wholly successful night attack by the FAA on the Italian Fleet at Taranto, 10/1/41, in HMS EAGLE.

GRIFFITHS (Glyn Walter Thomas). CONWAY 1933/35.

MiD. No details found.

GROVES (John). CONWAY 1939/40. Midshipman, RNR.

MiD: 26/5/44. For courage and skill in dangerous minesweeping operations in HMS POOLE.

HAES (Arthur Ernest). CONWAY NK. Wing Commander, RAF.

OBE: 28/12/45. He had been promoted to Wing Commander in 10/12/40.

HAES (Edward Mount). CONWAY 1911/13. Commander, RN.

DSC: 5/6/42. For outstanding zeal, patience and cheerfulness and for never failing to set an example of wholehearted devotion to duty.

KING HAAKON VII FREEDOM CROSS: 11/4/47. Presented to Acting Captain Haes, DSC, RN, for services connected to the liberation of Norway.

HAIGH (John Noel Fisher). CONWAY 1916/18. Commander (E), RN.

MiD: 25/6/43. For courage, leadership and skill.

HAILSTONE (William Blaxland Ernest). CONWAY NK. Lieutenant-Commander, RNR.

DSC: 13/11/42. For bravery in action and under fire at Tobruk.

HAINSWORTH (Derek Milner). CONWAY 1940/42. Midshipman, RNR.

DSC: 6/6/44. Successful actions against U-Boats while on convoy escort duty. U-91, U-358 and U-392 sunk. The Group ships were HM Ships AFFLECK, DAHLIA, GARLES, GORE, GOULD, HURRICANE and SPEY. They were part of the North Atlantic Escort Group.

HALBERT (William Edward). CONWAY NK. Lieutenant-Commander, RNR.

MiD. There are three MiDs. For good service in minesweeping operations. For minefield clearance. During the Normandy, Operation Neptune. During Dunkirk he served in HMS SUTTON. He attained the rank of Lieutenant-Commander.

DSC: 9/5/44. Minesweeping in support of Western Desert. Minesweeping almost continuously throughout the War, commanding ROMNEY, WHITEHAVEN, POSTILLION, and might have commanded the corvette MARIGOLD for eight months in 1942 (doubtful). Invalided out 6/4/47.

HALE (John William). CONWAY 1920/22. Lieutenant-Commander, RN.

DSO: 16/5/41. Outstanding courage and skill in a brilliant and wholly successful attack by the Fleet Air Arm on the Italian fleet at Taranto. Hale was Commanding Officer of 819 Squadron, February 1940-January 1941, in HMS ILLUSTRIOUS.

HALFHIDE (NK). CONWAY 1903/05. Captain, RN.
CBE: 2/1/40. Naval Officer in Charge of ISLE OF MAN, September 1944 to July 1945.

HALL (Charles Edward). CONWAY 1921/23. Acting Lieutenant-Commander, RD, RNR.
MiD (1): 10/11/44. For gallantry, determination and undaunted devotion to duty during the landing of Allied Forces on the coast of Normandy.
MiD (2): 22/12/44. For gallantry and outstanding service in the face of the enemy and for zeal, patience and cheerfulness in dangerous waters and for setting an example for outstanding devotion to duty, upholding the high standard of the traditions of the Royal Navy.

HALL (Thomas George Stanley). CONWAY 1916/18. Temporary Lieutenant, RNVR.
MiD: 1/6/44. For gallantry and outstanding service in the face of the enemy and for zeal, patience and cheerfulness in dangerous waters and for setting an example for outstanding devotion to duty, upholding the high standard of the traditions of the Royal Navy. Where was a 44 year old Lieutenant, RNVR, serving with such distinction?

HALLET (Alan Ritson). CONWAY NK. Lieutenant, RN.

DSC: 2/10/42. For bravery and skill in air operations in the Middle East.

HAMILTON (Timothy Walker Beamish Pollock). CONWAY NK. Lieutenant, RNR.

MiD: 21/11/41. For determination and skill in action against enemy submarines. Record shows HYDRANGEA (Lieutenant J E Woolfenden) sank U-401 on 3/8/41 in North Atlantic.

DSC. No record found.

Lieutenant T W B P Hamilton, DSC, RNR, shown as Commanding Officer of HMS CLARKIA from 7/3/45.

HARRISON BROADLEY (John). CONWAY NK. Acting Squadron Leader, RAF.

MiD. No details.

DFC: 29/8/41. While leading an attack on enemy destroyers near Pantellaria, one engine was hit and caught fire; the attack pressed, but both engines failed; bombs hit a target ship before the aircraft went into the sea. He was reported missing. No. 82 Squadron (Blenheims). He survived.

Transferred to the Reserve in November 1945. National Front parliamentary candidate 1973. Died of cancer after voluntarily piloting an aircraft through the fall-out of UK's first atomic bomb.

HARTLEY (Robert Victor). CONWAY 1931/33. Third Officer, Merchant Navy.

MiD: 30/7/43. For brave conduct when his ship encountered enemy ships, submarines, aircraft or mines. One of a long list of recipients of MN Commendations.

HAUGHTON (Wilfred John). CONWAY NK. Temporary Lieutenant, RNVR.

DSC: 5/5/44. For great skill, endurance and devotion to duty in clearing enemy minefields to enable supply convoys and bombardment forces to operate in support of the 8th Army in their advance from Egypt to Tunis. Attached to HMS BOSTON.

BAR to DSC. For courage and skill in dangerous minesweeping operations for Operation Antidote.

HAYES (Godfrey Harry). CONWAY 1936/38. Probably Acting Sub-Lieutenant, RNR.

DSC: 27/12/42. For courageous and continuous good service in the Channel Mobile Balloon Barrage. Transferred to the Canadian Navy in 1942. HMS GATINAIS (ex-French ship). Hayes was the Navigating Officer.

HAYMAN (James William). CONWAY NK. Chief Petty Officer, RN.

MiD: 23/1/42. For skill and enterprise in action against enemy submarines serving in HMS MARIGOLD.

HAYWARD (Peter William). CONWAY 1939/40. Lieutenant, RNR.

MiD: 13/7/45. For exceptional skill, courage and resource while serving in HMS EKINS in an action in which two explosive motor boats and a midget submarine were destroyed and later for his good work in damage control and bringing the ship safely to port after being torpedoed. HMS EKINS was a Captain Class Frigate.

HEWITT (Eric). CONWAY 1919/21. Captain, RD, RNR.

MiD: 19/11/43. For courage and endurance in defence against enemy air attacks while serving in HM Ships SHOREHAM, HYTHE and RYE on convoy escort duty. Commander Hewitt was in command. Captain E. Hewitt, RD, RNR, was the Captain Superintendent of CONWAY.

HIGGINS (Francis Bernard). CONWAY 1914/15. Chief Inspector of Mines.

OBE: 4/6/46. In the Colonial Mines Service on the Gold Coast.

HILL (Joseph Sterndale de Montclare). CONWAY 1935/36. Lieutenant, RN.

DSC: 29/12/42. For gallantry and outstanding service in the face of the enemy. Minesweeping in North Russia, HMS HALCYON.

BAR to DSC. No details found.

HILTON (Frederick William). CONWAY NK. Squadron Leader, RAF.

AFC: 11/10/40. Nothing found.

HOCART (George Collas). CONWAY 1923/24. Lieutenant, RNR.

DSC: 19/3/43. For bravery, skill and resolution while minesweeping in North Russian waters when in command of HMS HAZARD.

HOPPER (Peter Nelson). CONWAY 1935/37. Midshipman, RNR.

MiD: 1/8/41. For coolness, skill and enterprise when an Italian Convoy and its escorts were sunk between Sicily and Tripoli. He served in HMS NUBIA.

HULSE (Neil Sidney). CONWAY 1935/37. Second Officer, Merchant Navy.

MBE: 15/1/43. The ship was incessantly attacked for five days ... hit by bombs, abandonment was ordered. The ship's Anti-Aircraft defence was in the charge of the Second Officer and the ship put up a fine defence. The vessel was the EMPIRE LAWRENCE, (a CAM ship).

HUNT (Eric George Guilding). CONWAY NK. Commander, RIN.

DSC: 31/8/45. For outstanding service in coastal operation in the Red Sea which led to the capture of Massawa in April 1941, and the clearing of the harbour at Massawa.

HUNT (Frank William). CONWAY 1936/39. Lieutenant, RN.

MBE: 29/12/44. Hunt's occupation involved surveys and he supported landings in Sicily and the Mediterranean. He was part of the Hydrographic Survey Unit in the Mediterranean.

HUNT (George Edward). CONWAY 1930/32. Lieutenant-Commander, RN.

DSO*. There are no details of any of his awards
DSC*.
Mid*.
A noted submarine ACE during WW2, Hunt continued a long

career in the Royal Navy. CONWAY CLUB NEWSLETTER has printed a letter from 90-years old Captain Hunt describing the loss of HM S/M UNITY on 29/04/40. Unit:HM S/Ms UNITY, PROTEUS, ULTOR and Polish S/M SOKOL. This distinguished Old Conway and retired naval officer lives in Queensland.

HUNTER (William Kelly). CONWAY 1022/24. Lieutenant-Commander, RNR.

OBE. No trace of Gazette in this name, nor on any search sites. Two Gazettes found awarding RD October 1942 and promotion to Lieutenant-Commander in May.

HUTCHINGS (Frank Goddard). CONWAY 1918/20. Lieutenant-Commander, RD, RCNR.

MiD: 8/1/44. This Officer stands out as an excellent example of a good Commanding Officer. Keen, capable, energetic, hard-working he radiates an atmosphere of cheerful efficiency wherever he goes; and his unswerving devotion to duty is in the highest traditions of the Service. Hutchings was Commanding Officer of HMCS WESTMOUNT in Canadian waters. He served continually in minesweepers throughout the war.

HUTCHINGS (Kenhelm Jocelyn Townshend). CONWAY 1916/19. Commander, RD, RNR.

CROIX de GUERRE. No trace of this award.

MiD: 14/11/44. For gallantry, skill, determination and undaunted devotion to duty during the landing of Allied Forces on the coast of Normandy.

INNIS (Aubrey Richard de Lisle). CONWAY 1933/35. Wing Commander, RAF.

DFC: 6/7/43. No. 248 Squadron. No. 248 Squadron (Blenheims and Mosquito long range fighters) in Coastal Command. Retired as Wing Commander.

MiD. Gazette not found.

IRVINE (George Walter Alexander Thomas). CONWAY NK. Commander, RNR.

DSC: 28/5/43. For gallantry and outstanding service in the face of the enemy ... without which the high tradition of the Royal Navy could not have been upheld.

MiD. Commander Irvine commanded three Bangor class mine-sweepers from August 1941 to February 1945, being awarded the DSC in the last named. HM Ships FRASERBURGH, ROMNEY or WHITEHAVEN.

IRVING (Robert Beaufin). CONWAY 1890/92. Captain, RD, RNR.

OBE: 29/7/19. For valuable services in Naval Transport, as Officer-in-Charge landing military stores on the Palestine coast. Unit: C in C Mediterranean Staff. This award is on WW One Honours Board.

KB: 28/5/43. Commodore Captain Cunard-White Star, Ltd. Sir Robert Irving (1877-1954) inherited the family home 'Bonshaw'.

JENNINGS (William John). CONWAY 1937/39. Midshipman, RNR.

DSC: 6/2/42. For bravery and endurance minesweeping under attack from enemy aircraft. Since he lost his life before this award was gazetted, he possibly died without knowing he had been honoured. He was serving in HMS SOTRA (M/S Whaler) in the Mediterranean. Midshipman W J Jennings, DSC, RNR, lost his life in BARHAM, 25/11/41.

JOHNSON (John). CONWAY 1887/89. Rank unknown
DSC. Nothing found, WW One or Two. He was possibly Master (aged mid-to-late-sixties).

KEAY (Stanley Walter). CONWAY NK. Chief Officer, Merchant Navy.
OBE: 23/1/44. Ship was attacked by enemy aircraft, caught fire and was lost. A very long citation regarding a ship on fire in convoy, during which the Chief Officer acted with great gallantry, only leaving the ship when she finally foundered in the Mediterranean.

KING (Frederic Geoffrey). CONWAY 1921/23. Temporary Lieutenant, RNR.
MiD: 27/6/41. For outstanding zeal, patience and cheerfulness, and never failing to set an example of whole-hearted devotion to duty.

KNIBBS (Richard Burden). CONWAY 1922/24. Lieutenant, RA.
MiD: 27/4/45. The award may have been posthumous; no record found. He was killed in action in Italy in 1944 and was buried in the Florence War Cemetery.

KNIGHT (George Douglas). CONWAY NK. Third Officer, Merchant Navy.
MiD: 5/2/43. For gallantry, skill and resolution while an

important convoy was fought through to Malta in the face of relentless attacks by day and night from enemy aircraft, submarines and surface forces. This was Operation Pedestal.

LABEY (George Thomas). CONWAY 1902/04. Army(WW One) and Pilot (WW Two).
MC: 28/12/17. There was no specific citation. In 1920, he became an Acting Captain, RE, a rank which he was to retain.
MBE: 4/6/46. Bengal Pilot Service.

LAING (Ian Horace). CONWAY 1930/32. Temporary Sub-Lieutenant, RNR
DSC: Post 42. Nothing found. Navy lists him as Commanding Officer of Schooner TIBERIO as part of the Western Desert Service.

LANE (Harry Robertson). CONWAY 1900? Commodore, RNR.
OBE: 2/6/43. Ocean Convoys. Entered RNR as Lieutenant in 1924.

LAWRENCE (Charles James). CONWAY 1921/23. Squadron Leader, RAFVR.
MiD. No details.
OBE: 28/12/45.

LEARMONT (Percy Hewitt). CONWAY 1910/12. Captain, RIM.
CIE: 4/6/46. Mentioned as a much respected investigating officer in the Indian Navy 'mutiny' of 1946. Thirty-five years

service, including two wars, deserves recognition! Died at the age of 91 years.

LEIGH (Thomas Edwin Shea). CONWAY 1935/37. Midshipman, RNR.

MiD: 28/6/40. For daring, resource and devotion to duty in the Second Battle of Narvik. ICARUS was an 'I' Class Fleet destroyer equipped to lay mines. It was a commendation for Brave Conduct for assisting the Police in making an arrest.

L'ESTRANGE (Henry Owen). CONWAY 1926/29. Lieutenant, RNR.

DSC: 4/1/42. Involved with capture of U-570 in HMS KINGSTON AGATE, (A/S Trawler) in Northern waters. Commander H O L'Estrange, RD, DSC, RNR, (Commodore Royal Fleet Auxiliary) died 'in harness' in Singapore, December 1972.

LETTY (Angus). CONWAY 1930s. Captain, RNR.

DSC: 5/7/40. A minelaying operation.

DSO: 26/3/43. For distinguished services. Letty was attached to the Naval Intelligence Division. Captain, RNR, 31/12/59.

LING (John Thurston). CONWAY NK. Master, Merchant Navy.

OBE: 9/1/45. Outstanding coolness and courage. All 66 crew survived. ADVISER was torpedoed in darkness in Indian Ocean, crew safely abandoned ship in boats. Captain re-boarded and eventually, together with the crew, prevented ship from sinking; taken in tow and thus saved. SS ADVISER, Charente Steamship Co (T & J Harrison).

LOCK (Geoffrey Dalls). CONWAY 1902/05. Chief Air Raid Warden.

MBE: 29/12/44. Chief Air Raid Warden, Civil Defence Bath.

LOGIE (George Malcolm). CONWAY 1039/41. Captain, R S Fusiliers.

MiD: 6/6/45. No details found.

McCULLUM (Daniel). CONWAY 1903/05. Flight Sergeant, RAAF.

BEM: 5/6/42. A Flight Sergeant D MacCullum, DFM, AAF, was mentioned in despatches in Gazette 35586 (2524) in Birthday Honours. He would have been 50-55 years of age.

MacGREGOR (Ivor Gregor). CONWAY 1908/10. Merchant Navy.

MiD. No information. Would have been in his fifties, possibly ship's Master.

MARE (Phillip Armitage). CONWAY 1905/07. Commodore, RIN.

CIE: 8/6/45. Captain P A Mare is shown in command of HMIS SUTLEJ at Belfast and Madras during hostilities. He was the Chief of Administration, RIN, HQ. SUTLEJ was a Black Swan sloop.

MARRIOTT (George Brian). CONWAY NK. Temporary Lieutenant, RNR.

MiD: 30/4/43. For bravery, endurance and devotion to

duty in North African waters. He served in HM Tug ST. DAY in Gibraltar.

MARTIN (Alistair Angus). CONWAY 1918/20. Commander, RD, RNR.

MiD (1): 4/10/40. For courage and devotion to duty when ship attacked by enemy aircraft in HM M/S Trawler TAIPO.

DSC: 31/12/40. Outstanding zeal, patience and cheerfulness for never failing to set an example of devotion to duty without which the high tradition of the Royal Navy could not have been upheld.

MiD (2): 27/3/42. Courage, skill and endurance while minesweeping in the Mediterranean.

BAR to DSC: 3/12/43. For courage and devotion to duty in minesweeping operations. Commander Martin was now the Commanding Officer of HMS ROTHSAY in the Mediterranean.

MiD (3): 10/11/44. Courage and devotion to duty minesweeping in the Mediterranean in HMS ROTHSAY.

SECOND BAR to DSC: 23.3.45. For distinguished service and gallantry during the invasion of Southern France. Commanding Officer of HMS ROTHSAY.

MARTIN (John Dennis). CONWAY 1928/30. Lieutenant, RN.

DSC: 14/5/43. For successful patrols in submarines. One of two submariner brothers who formed a unique partnership.

BAR to DSC: 14/12/45. Courage, efficiency and devotion to duty whilst serving in HM Submarines in aggressive operations against Japanese shipping, often performed in shallow waters and in the face of serious opposition. Joe

Martin was the Commanding Officer of HM S/M SOLENT in the Gulf of Siam.

MARTIN (Kenneth Henry). CONWAY 1935/37. Lieutenant, RN.

DSC: 14/12/45. Courage, efficiency and devotion to duty whilst serving in HM Submarines in aggressive operations against Japanese shipping, often performed in shallow waters and in the face of serious opposition in HM S/M SLEUTH in the Gulf of Siam. Partnered his brother J D (Joe) Martin Commanding Officer of SOLENT in remarkable teaming.

MARTIN-LEAK (Cecil William Rhodes). CONWAY 1937/39. Lieutenant, 2nd Dragoons.

MC. No citation found. He served in the Royal Armoured Corps in Germany and was buried in Becklingen War Cemetery, 1945.

MATHESON (Roderick Lees). CONWAY 1923/25. Lieutenant-Commander, RN.

DSC. Nothing found.

MAUNDRELL (Arthur Goodall). CONWAY 1899/1900. Merchant Navy.

MiD. Would have been late fifties; probably a Master.

MAWSON (Vivian Adams). CONWAY NK. Temporary Lieutenant, RNVR.

MiD: 19/1/45. For courage and skill in minesweeping operations in the approaches to Le Havre.

McREYNOLDS (John Bernard). CONWAY NK. Acting Temporary Lieutenant-Commander, RNR.

DSC: 19/5/44. For outstanding courage, resolution, leadership, skill, and devotion to duty in HM Ships in operations which led to successful landings on the Italian mainland at Salerno.

McVEY (Thomas). CONWAY 1931/33. Lieutenant, RNR.

MiD: 26/9/41. For good services in operations off the coast of Italian East Africa in HMS HAWKINS

MILLER (John Isdale). CONWAY 1917/19. Lieutenant-Commander, RD, RNR.

DSO: 28/4/40. For exemplary enterprise, zeal, leadership and resource in Anti-Submarine Trawlers and untiring endeavours to harass the enemy in HM Trawler BLACKFLY in home waters.

DSC: 30/5/41. Gallantry and distinguished services in the withdrawal from the beaches of Greece and in face of many and great difficulties and helped to save many thousands of troops of the Allied Armies. Probably in HMS SALVIA.

BAR to DSC: 6/1/42. For outstanding gallantry, fortitude and resolution during the Battle of Crete in HMS SALVIA. HMS SALVIA, (Lieutenant-Commander J. I. Miller, RD, DSO, DSC*.), was torpedoed and lost with all hands, 24/12/41.

MILLER (Robert Stevenson). CONWAY NK. Lieutenant-Commander, RNR.

DSC: 9/7/40. Good service in the Royal Navy since the outbreak of the war in HMS LYNX, attached to the Minesweeping Base in Dover.

MiD: 27/8/40. For good services in operations off the Dutch, Belgian and French coasts. HMS KEITH was sunk by Stuka dive-bombers off Dunkirk on 1/6/40.
Lieutenant-Commander R. S. Miller was wounded when HMS TWEED was torpedoed and sunk SW of Ireland, July 1944.

MILNE-HENDERSON (Thomas Maxwell Stuart). CONWAY 1903/05. Commodore, RIM.
OBE: 2/4/05. Several Gazettes chart his move from 'Major RE' to 'Lieutenant RIM' and the OBE is mentioned. After entries for 1919, he was appointed as Commander of Marine Survey, RIN, in 1937.
CIE: 27/6/41. Commodore Milne-Henderson retired.

MONRO (Kenneth Stanley). Conway 1915/18. Lieutenant-Commander, RD, RNR.
OBE: 7/12/45. For distinguished service during the war in Europe on Convoy Duties.

MOORE (George Dunbar). CONWAY 1908/10. Rear-Admiral, RAN.
CBE: 31/12/43. Commanded at least two cruisers during WW Two. Rear Admiral Moore died in 1979.

MOORHOUSE (Arthur). CONWAY 1920/22. Lieutenant, RCNR.
MiD: 28/5/43. 'This officer has been in continuous command of HMC Ships since spring 1940 and has, at all times, conducted himself with unfailing cheerfulness and devotion to duty'. Served in HMCS SHEDIAC, (Flower Class), and SAULT ST. MARIE.

MORGAN (Sir Charles Eric). CONWAY 1901/02. Vice-Admiral, RN.

DSO. There are no details, apart from his promotion to Lieutenant, RN, 11/10/11.

MiD: 5/3/20. For valuable services in Northern European waters.

MiD: 30/1/42. For bravery and enterprise in the Battle of Matapan in HMS VALIANT in the Mediterranean.

CB: 29/12/44. Rear-Admiral C E Morgan, DSO, RN, was Flag Officer in Charge of HMS BALDUR.

KCB: 4/6/46. He was involved with Naval Personnel and was the Admiral Commanding Reserves. His speciality was navigation.

MORGAN (Geoffrey). CONWAY NK. Lieutenant-Commander, RD, RNR.

DSC. No details found, although he had been awarded the DSC when he was given his RD. HMS STAG, Crete.

MORTIMER (William Wyndham). CONWAY 1920/22. Acting Temporary Lieutenant-Commander, RNR.

MiD: 11/12/42. For gallantry and devotion to duty at Singapore.

MBE: 4/6/46. No detail.

MOULD (Peter William Olbert). CONWAY 1932/33. Squadron Leader, RAF.

DFC: 16/7/40. For operational flying. Was reputed to have shot down the first enemy aircraft of the war.

BAR to DFC: 9/9/41. A long citation including '... magnificent example and courage ..'. His squadron accounted for eight aircraft destroyed, fourteen probably destroyed and seven damaged in the Battle of Britain. Gained triple blue at RAF College, Cranwell.

Squadron Leader Mould was Killed in Action defending Malta, 1/10/1941.

MURRAY (Andrew Gerrard). CONWAY 1938/39. Sub-Lieutenant, RNR.

MiD: 13/4/45. Leadership, skill and daring in an attack on an enemy convoy.

MYERS (Leslie Brian). CONWAY 1914/17. Rank unknown.

MiD. Nothing found.

NEDWILL (Peter Anthony). CONWAY 1933/35. Lieutenant, RN.

MiD: 1/1/41. Killed in Action in HMS SHEFFIELD, 26/5/41. Chief Cadet Captain in CONWAY.

NEWBIGIN (Thomas Leslie). CONWAY 1929/31. Lieutenant. RNVR.

MiD: 8/1/42. Withdrawal from Crete in MTB 216, part of the 19th MTB Flotilla. Newbigin became an Admiralty Salvage Officer, having qualified as a mechanical engineer after CONWAY.

MBE: 1/1/46. HMS ODYSSEY, Admiralty Salvage Department.

O'BRIEN (Hubert John). CONWAY 1925/27. Flying Officer, RAF.

DFC: 1/12/44. No specific citation but the Squadron is quoted as patrolling the South Atlantic. No. 220 Squadron, (Liberators).

OGILVY (George). CONWAY 1937/39. Lieutenant (A), RN.

MiD: 23/3/45. For distinguished service and gallantry during the invasion of Southern France. He served in a RAF Fighter Squadron in the Mediterranean. Transferred to Lieutenant, (A), RN, 18/11/43, formerly RNR.

OLDROYD (Arthur Waite). CONWAY NK. Squadron Leader, RAF.

AFC: 31/12/40. For gallant conduct. A Gazette of September 1939 shows A W Oldroyd recalled from the reserve.

DFC: 19/5/42. A long citation referring to a raid on the Skoda works at Pilsen; it concludes 'displayed skill and courage of a high standard which largely contributed to the safe return of his aircraft and crew'. Squadron Leader Oldroyd served in Bomber Command in Europe. Nos. 49 or 50 Squadron.

PAINTER (Douglas Francom). CONWAY 1910/11. Commander, RN, (Retd).

DSC. Listed as D F Painter, DSC. Probably retired pre-war and re-employed, but can find no record.

PARIS (George William). CONWAY 30/32. Colonel. Indian Army.

MiD. Indian Army Engineers. No other detail.

MBE: 15/1/46. For gallant and distinguished services in Burma. Colonel George W Paris died December 1998.

PASSMORE-EDWARDS (Henry Ellis). CONWAY 1913/15. Lieutenant-Commander, RINR.

MiD: 6/3/42. For courage, enterprise and devotion to duty in operations in the Persian Gulf in HMIS LAWRENCE (Minesweeping Sloop).

PEATE (Henry Benjamin). CONWAY 1926/27. Captain, RD, RNR.

MiD. Commanding Officer of HMS PRINS ALBERT. Mentioned in Despatches four times.

DSC: 21/12/43. Operation 'Husky'. Excellent write-up in the reference, including photographs. Suffered burns after a fire in his ship. He took up tapestry to keep his fingers supple, and remained an active needle man thereafter! Retired as Captain, RNR.

PEIRSE (Sir Richard Edmund Charles). CONWAY 1906/08. Air Chief Marshal, RAF.

DSO: Before May 1915. He is gazetted as 'seeing much action along the Belgian coast, attacking submarine bases' whilst serving in the RFC (Naval Wing).

AFC: 31/12/18. He served in Bomber Command.

CROCE di GUERRA (Italy): 4/4/19. For services in the Mediterranean serving in the RFC (Naval Wing). Pierse was granted a commission as Flight Lieutenant, RAF, in 1920. His career had started when he was appointed Sub-Lieutenant, RNVR, 1/11/12. He held the rank of Lieutenant-Colonel, RFC, (RNAS).

KCB: 1/6/40. Air Marshall Sir Richard Edmund Charles Pierce, KCB, DSO, AFC, was the Air Officer in Command of Bomber Command, United Kingdom. He died in 1970.

PHILIPS (Percival Hutchinson). CONWAY 1919/20. Commander (E), RN.
OBE: 2/6/44. Some mystery about name … possibly CRAVEN-PHILLIPS.

PHILIPS (George). CONWAY 1920s/30s. Temporary Acting Lieutenant-Commander, RNVR.
DSC: 2/10/42. For daring and resolution while commanding the forces in the raid on Dieppe.
MiD: 10/11/44. For gallantry, skill, determination and undaunted devotion to duty during the landing of Allied Forces on the coast of Normandy.

PINCKNEY (Charles Wilfred Cecil). CONWAY NK. Lieutenant-Commander, RD, RNR.
OBE. He commanded HMS JENNET, a Boom Defence Vessel, in the Tobruk/Port Said area in 1941.

PIZEY (Charles Thomas Mark). CONWAY 1912/15. Captain, RN.
MiD. There are two mentions … December 1940 and 27/6/41. For outstanding zeal, patience and cheerfulness, and never failing to set an example of wholehearted devotion to duty without which the honour of the Royal Navy would not be upheld. Pizey was Captain (D), 21st DF, June 1940 to 1942.
DSO: 1/1/42. No details found.

CB: 27/3/42. Daring and fine judgement in leading a striking force of HM Destroyers against the German Battle Cruisers SCHARNHORST, GNEISENAU, and Cruiser PRINZ EUGEN.

BAR to DSO: 27/11/42. For gallantry, skill and resolution in HMS Ships escorting an important Convoy to North Russia in the face of relentless attack by enemy aircraft and submarines.

From December 1943 to 1945, DOO the Admiralty. 1945-46, CoS to C in C Home Fleet (Nelson).

POOLE (James Malcolm Stuart). CONWAY 1935/36. Lieutenant, RN.

DSC: 28/11/41. Outstanding bravery, skill and resolution on successful submarine patrols in HM S/M URGE in the Mediterranean.

BAR to DSC: 25/9/42. For bravery and devotion to duty on successful submarine patrols. URGE sank and damaged several Italian Navy heavy and light units. URGE was lost in April-May 1942.

PRESTON (Henry Francis Morrison). CONWAY 1919/21. Lieutenant, RNR.

MiD. Nothing found, but he spent most of the war minesweeping.

DSC: 7/12/43. For steadfast courage and skill in dangerous and important minesweeping operations.

PRETTY (Francis Cecil). CONWAY 1904/07. Master, Merchant Navy.

DSC. No record found in London Gazette other than OBE and DSC (WW One).

OBE: 31/1/41. Vessel struck by bombs and ship/cargo saved ... a long citation, but the name of ship and whereabouts not stated. Possibly a Malta Convoy. Memorial Board states that he was lost in MV NOTTINGHAM, 7/11/1941.

DSO. Could this have been posthumous? MV NOTTINGHAM fought back and tried to ram the attacking U-Boat.

PRIM (Thomas Mark). CONWAY NK. Temporary Sub-Lieutenant, RNR.

MiD: 10/12/43. For outstanding service in fire-fighting after an explosion.

PULVERCRAFT (William Godfrey). CONWAY 1917/19. Commander(E), RN.

OBE: 28/5/43. No details known.

RATTRAY (Arthur Rullion). CONWAY 1904/06. Rear-Admiral, RIN.

CIE. No details known.

CB: 8/6/45. Flag Officer in charge Bombay.

REVILL (David Haigh). CONWAY NK. Lieutenant, RNR.

DSC: 11/9/42. For bravery and skill while serving in HMS WILD SWAN (modified S destroyer). His ship was attacked by twelve German dive bombers on 17/6/42 and sunk, but not before six aircraft had been shot down. This action was in the Atlantic and it was a remarkable achievement for a ship on her own.

ROBERTS (David Neal). CONWAY 1920/22. Air Commodore, RAF.

AFC. Always listed in Gazette with AFC, but no citation found.

OBE: 23/9/41. For distinguished service rendered in operational commands of the RAF from 1st October 1940 to 31st March 1941. He was a Wing Commander at this stage in the war.

CBE: 20/12/53.

ROBINSON (Basil Vernon). CONWAY 1928/29. Group Captain, RAF.

AFC. Mentioned in Gazettes, but no entry found for this award. Date unknown.

DFC. No details.

BAR to DFC: 5/1/43. In November 1942, during a raid on Turin, a dangerous fire broke out ... he ordered his crew to bale out, then, single handed, he flew his four-engined bomber across the Alps and returned safely to base. There is long citation at reference. His unit was No. 35 Squadron.

DSO: 6/1/42. For the December 1941 attack on GNEISNAU and SCHARNHORST at Brest.

Group Captain B. V. Robinson, DSO, DFC*, AFC, RAF, was Killed in Action over Berlin in 1943 aged 31.

ROBINSON (David). CONWAY 1937/39. Third Officer, Merchant Navy.

COMMENDATION (Posthumous): 10/8/45. EMPIRE JAVELIN, a Landing Ship Infantry, was on passage from Portsmouth to Le Havre on 28/12/44 when she was torpedoed and sunk. Citation: 'Brave conduct when their ship encountered enemy ships, aircraft, submarines or mines.' SS EMPIRE JAVELIN, (Blue Star).

ROGERS (John Cecil Kelly). CONWAY 1919/21. Captain. Civil Air Transport.

OBE: 31/12/40. Captain Kelly Rogers was a pioneer civil air transport pilot. He is listed on the Conway web-site under 'notable Old Conways'. Flew Churchill from Plymouth to Bermuda in 1942. British Overseas Airways Corporation. Civil aviation (flying boats). Captain J C Kelly Rogers OBE, FRAeS, born 1905. Became first Chief Pilot of Aer Lingus.

ROSOMAN (Richard Robert Loane). CONWAY 1920/22. Lieutenant-Commander, RNR.

MiD: 31/12/40. HMS TIERCEL (Armed Yacht: Boarding Vessel) in Home Waters.

RUMP (Frederick John (always listed as Fred Rump)). CONWAY 1927/29. Air Commodore, RAF.

OBE: 2/6/44.

RUSSELL FLINT (Francis Murray). CONWAY 1933/35. Lieutenant, RNVR.

MiD: 12/6/42. For gallantry, steadfastness and devotion to duty in HMS THANET in a night action with a superior Japanese force. THANET (S Class destroyer) was sunk in action 27/1/42 off the East coast of Malaya.
A professional artist, RF painted the honours board after the war!

SABINE (Charles Wheatstone). CONWAY 1913/15. Commander, RN.

OBE: 1940. While in command of HM Surveying ship FRANKLIN in support of minelaying operations 1939/41, Dover Strait to Faeroes.

SALTER (Douglas Collier). CONWAY NK. Lieutenant, RN.

MiD: 4/10/40. For gallantry and devotion to duty in operations in Norway in HMS HOOD.

SAMPSON (Charles David). CONWAY NK. Lieutenant-Commander, RNVR.

DSC: 3/12/43. For steadfast courage and skill in a dangerous and important minesweeping operation while serving in HMS POLRUAN in the Mediterranean.

MiD: 10/11/44. For minesweeping operations in the Mediterranean in HMS POLRUAN (Commanding Officer February 1943 to January 1945). Lieutenant-Commander C D Sampson, VRD, DSC, RNVR on Retired List, 4/2/48.

SANDERS (Harry Marcus Crews). CONWAY 1916/18. Lieutenant Commander, RNR.

DSC: 12/11/40. On 1/7/40, U-26 was scuttled after being damaged by eight depth charges from GLADIOLUS and bombs from an RAAF Sunderland. The U-boat crew survived and made prisoner. North Atlantic.

DSO: 5/9/41. For enterprise, skill and devotion to duty in action against enemy submarines. On 27/6/41, U-556 (Herbert Wohlfarth) was sunk by depth charges from HMS NASTURTIUM, CELENDINE and GLADIOLUS. Five dead and forty one survivors off U-556. GLADIOLUS was lost with all hands while picking up survivors, having been torpedoed by U-558, 17/10/41.

SAREL (John Charles). CONWAY 1929/32. RAF.

DFC. Nothing found.

SARGENT (Paul). CONWAY NK. Commander, RNR.

MiD: 17/12/43. Gallant and distinguished services and untiring devotion to duty which led to the capture of Sicily by Allied Forces.

DSC: 28/3/45. Distinguished service and gallantry during the invasion of Southern France.

SAUNDERS (James Begg). CONWAY 1925/27. Lieutenant-Commander, RN.

MiD: 14/1/44. For gallant and distinguished service in HM Ships NELSON, WARSPITE, RODNEY, VALIANT, etc., in operations in the Mediterranean from the time of the entry of Italy into the war until the surrender of the Italian fleet.

SCOTT (David?). CONWAY NK. Lieutenant, RN.

MiD. Light Coastal Forces.

DSC: 10/12/43. For gallant and distinguished services in an attack on enemy Merchant Shipping while serving in Light Coastal Craft in Home waters and Mediterranean.

SHARMAN (Henry Clare). CONWAY NK. Temporary Lieutenant, RNR.

MiD: 31/12/43. Zeal, patience and cheerfulness in dangerous waters, and for setting an example of whole-hearted devotion to duty, upholding the high tradition of the Royal Navy.

SIMMS (Charles E). CONWAY 1912/14. Commander (E), RN.

DSO: 20/2/40. By his zeal and energy, brought his engines

to full power in record time, and his thorough knowledge of the ship and perfect organisation … checked the damage. His calm and cheerful manner set a fine example to his fellows. HMS EXETER in the Battle of the River Plate.

SIVEWRIGHT (Robert Henry Vivian). CONWAY 1907/09. Commander, RN.

MiD: 1/1/41. For wholehearted devotion to duty without which the high tradition of the Royal Navy could not have been upheld.

DSC: 27/3/42. For courage, skill and endurance while minesweeping in dangerous waters in HM Ships BANGOR, BLYTHE, EASTBOURNE, ILFRACOMBE, PETERHEAD, POLRUAN, ROTHSAY and SIDMOUTH. The 9th Minesweeping Flotilla off the Belgian coast.

SMITH (Frank). CONWAY 1921/23. Temporary Lieutenant(E), RNR.

DSC: 28/5/43. For gallantry and outstanding service in the face of the enemy.

SMITH (Vivian Funge). CONWAY NK. Commander, RNR.

DSO:1/8/41. For enterprise and skill in action against enemy U-Boats. Internet has a good account of the capture of U-110 resulting in acquisition of German codes. HMS AUBRETIA in the North Atlantic. Commander V F Smith, RD, DSO, RNR, was in command of HMS EVENLODE July 1944-May 1945.

SMITH (Peter). Aka **DUGGAN-SMITH.** CONWAY NK. Squadron Leader, RAF.

DFC. 1940. No. 113 Squadron.

SMYTHE (John Patrick). CONWAY 1923/25. Lieutenant-Commander, RNR.
DSC: 10/12/43. For gallantry in action in HM Ships STORK and STONECROP

STEPHEN (John Andrew William). CONWAY 1929/30. Squadron Leader, RAF.
DFC: 20/2/40. No citation. No. 107 Squadron (Blenheims).
BAR to DFC: 22/12/40. No citation given.
MiD: 1/8/47. Appointed to a Permanent Commission and promoted to Squadron Leader.

STEPHENSON (John Keith Burdett). CONWAY 1916/17. Commander, RN.
MiD: 28/6/40. For daring, resource and devotion to duty in the Second Battle of Narvik. HMS WARSPITE.
OBE. Commander Stephenson probably listed after the end of the war.

STEWART (John Parker). CONWAY NK. Lieutenant-Commander, RNR.
MiD: 3/10/41. For good services against enemy submarines in HMS ARABIS in the North Atlantic.
DSC: 2/1/42. For skill and enterprise in action against enemy submarines, whilst in command of HMS ARABIS (Corvette) sank U-651, 29/6/41.

STRIDE (Desmond Adair). CONWAY 1902/04. Commander, RN.

MiD: 16/8/40. For good services in the withdrawal of the Allied Armies from the beaches at Dunkirk.

STUDD (Theodore Quintus). CONWAY 1909/11. Group Captain, RAF.
MiD: 1/1/45.
DFC. ' … 60 successful bombing raids ... skilful pilot ... no matter what adverse conditions may prevail.'

STURDY (Walter Ronald Nisbet). CONWAY 1932/34. Squadron Leader, RAF.
DFC. No details.
BAR to DFC: 12/1/43. No. 214 Squadron in European bomber operations.

SUTCLIFFE (George Ernest). CONWAY 1899/1901. Commander, RN.
MiD: 24/11/44. For distinguished service in operations which led to the successful landing of Allied Forces in Europe.

SWIFT (Donald Holmes). CONWAY 1931/33. Lieutenant, RN.
MiD (1): 3/9/40. For services on the occasion of the loss of HMS DUNOON. DUNOON was mined and sunk 25 nautical miles ENE of Great Yarmouth.
DSC: 14/11/41. For courage, resolution and skill in minesweeping. HMS CROMER in UK waters.
BAR to DSC: 10/11/44. For courage and determination in a series of successful attacks on enemy escorted convoys off the coast of France. HMS BELLONA.

MiD (2): 24/11/44. Gallantry, skill, determination and undaunted devotion to duty during the landing of Allied Forces on the coast of Normandy. HMS BELLONA.

TAYLOR (Charles William). CONWAY 1927/30. Lieutenant-Commander, RNR.

DSC. Date unknown. RD awarded to Lieutenant-Commander C W Taylor, DSC, RNR, 4/3/47. He was a submariner and commanded VAMPIRE until the end of the war, mainly in Aegean and Greek waters.

TAYLOR (Ralph Palmer). CONWAY 1919/21. Lieutenant-Colonel, Indian Army.

MiD: 23/11/43. 17th Dogra Regiment.

THELWELL (Robert George). CONWAY NK. Commander, RD, RNR.

OBE: 1/1/41. Details unknown.

THOMAS (Allan). CONWAY NK. Lieutenant, SASDF.

DSC: 5/9/41. For courage, resolution and devotion to duty in the face of enemy air attacks in command of HMSAS SOUTHERN SEA, which was damaged in an air attack at Tobruk. SASDF provided a flotilla of ex-whalers for minesweeping in N Africa.

THOMAS (Peter Hugh). CONWAY 1937/39. Sub-Lieutenant, RNR.

MiD: 18/9/42. For bravery and resolution while escorting HM Ships … an important convoy to Malta. He served in HMS ITHURIEL … Operation Harpoon. In 1985 he was listed as Captain P H Thomas, RD.

THORNTON (Frederick Harold). CONWAY NK. Lieutenant-Commander, RNR.

OBE: 13/3/42. Commanding Officer of LORD LLOYD, (A/S Trawler), 1940 and PIMPERNEL, (Corvette), 1942.

DSC. This had been awarded when he received his RD, 7/7/44. Very much involved in the Western Approaches. He became a Union Castle Captain.

THORNYCROFT (Charles Edward Mytton). CONWAY 1934/36. Lieutenant-Commander, RN.

MiD (3). Operations in the Aegean Sea.

TIDSWELL (Frederick George). CONWAY 1918/20. Lieutenant-Commander, RNZNVR.

DSC. No details.

MiD. Gazette awards MiD for 'Great bravery and devotion to duty.' This quotes Tidswell as having the DSC pre-7/42, in HMS ELGIN in Home Waters ... Minesweeping. ELGIN was mined and damaged, 4/5/44, and deemed not worth repairing.

TIMBRELL (Robert Walter). CONWAY 1935/37. Sub-Lieutenant, RCN.

DSC: 27/8/40. For good services in the withdrawal of Allied Armies from the beaches at Dunkirk in HMS LLANTHONY.

MiD (2): 1/8/44. U-Boat 621 was sunk in the Bay of Biscay, followed by U-984 two days later by a Canadian Escort Group. Possibly in HMCS OTTOWA.

TIPPETS (Harry Jeffreys). CONWAY 1938/40. Lieutenant, RNR.

DSO. No information on award, but after 1944. Chief Cadet Captain Summer Term 1940.

TREWEEK (Cecil Randolph). CONWAY 1900/01. Captain, RD, RNR.
OBE: 29/12/44. New Year Honours on recommendation of the Canadian Government. Employed by Imperial Oil, Co., since 1919 and Park Shipping. In command at sea throughout the war in dangerous waters and highly respected.

TURBETT (Cecil Lefroy). CONWAY 1910/12. Commander, RIN.
OBE: 9/7/40. In India.

TYLER (Charles Frederick). CONWAY 1920/23. Lieutenant, RNR.
MiD: 19/5/44. Outstanding courage, resolution, leadership, skill or devotion to duty in operations which led to successful landings on the Italian mainland at Salerno.

TYRER (Edward Austen). CONWAY 1930s. Lieutenant, RN.
DSC: 10/11/44. For courage and determination in a series of successful attacks on enemy convoys off the coast of France. Fourteen ships listed in one of which he would have been serving.

VEATOR (Alan). CONWAY NK. Lieutenant, RNR.
DSC: 15/6/45. For bravery, determination and devotion to duty while serving in HMS RETALICK and Light Coastal

Forces in operation against E-boats, enemy submarines, and explosive motor boats.

WALGATE (Richard). CONWAY 1928/30. Lieutenant, RNR.

MiD: 16/12/41. For good service in action against enemy submarines. On the 25ᵗʰ August, 1941, U-452 was sunk SE of Iceland by HM A/S Trawler VASACAMA.

WALKER (Edward John Raymond). CONWAY 1934/36. Sub-Lieutenant.

DSC: 13/11/42. For skill and resource in action against enemy submarines while serving in HM Ships PROTEA and SOUTHERN MAID. The Italian submarine ONDINA was sunk by Armed Trawlers PROTEA and SOUTHERN MAID working with Fleet Air Arm Walrus from No. 700 Squadron on 11/7/42 in the Eastern Mediterranean.

WATSON (Donald Eric Ogilvy). CONWAY 1928/31. Lieutenant, RN.

MiD: 7/5/40. Daring, endurance and resource in the conduct of hazardous and dangerous operations against the enemy in His Majesty's submarine HM S/M TRUANT in European Waters.

MiD: 8/8/41. For skill and enterprise in HM S/M TRUANT, 1940-41.

TRUANT was very active and successful in European waters under Hutchinson and Haggard.

DSC: 10/10/41. For courage and skill in successful submarine patrols. By 1941 TRUANT was operating in the Mediterranean.

Donald Watson was lost on 11/11/42 in HM S/M UNBEATEN.

WATSON (Douglas Rannie). CONWAY 1927/29. Lieutenant, RCNR.
MBE: 6/8/43. For outstanding leadership and enterprise in taking a boarding party aboard a sinking merchant vessel, rescuing crew members, and salvaging a motor launch she was carrying as deck cargo. The merchant vessel was HMCS MORDERN.

WATSON (John Raymond). CONWAY 1942/43. Midshipman, RNR.
MBE: 7/9/45. For courage and initiative when in charge of a boarding party sent from HMS LOCH MORE to board a captured German U-boat off the North of Scotland. When the U-Boat started to sink he mustered the party on deck, gave orders to abandon her, and kept the party together in the water until they were picked up.

WHAYMAN (Jackson). CONWAY NK. Commander, RNR.
MiD: 9/10/42. For good services on escort duty in HM Ships HAVELOCK and LAVENDER.
DSC: 21/1/44. For courage and unceasing devotion to duty landing reinforcements vitally important to the Army in crossing Volturno River in the Mediterranean.
BAR to DSC: 19/5/44. For outstanding courage, resolution and devotion to duty in operations which led to successful landings on the Italian mainland and at Salerno.
MiD: 6/11/44. For courage, skill, determination and

undaunted devotion to duty during the landing of Allied Forces in Normandy.

WHITE (Hedley Ian Saxton). CONWAY 1933/35. Lieutenant, RNR.

DSC: 7/12/45. For distinguished service during the war in Europe.

WHITE (William Douglas Stanley). CONWAY 1932/32. Lieutenant, RN.

MiD: 24/9/40. For services in or near Narvik in HMS PROTECTOR; she was a netlayer launched in 1936, designed to lay nets to protect the fleet.

WILCOX (William Harold Mortimer). CONWAY NK. Lieutenant-Colonel, RASC.

MBE: 9/7/40. In 1939 Wilcox rejoined from the Reserve of Officers of the RASC.

MiD: 14/9/43. For gallant and distinguished service in North Africa. He retired with honorary rank of Lieutenant Colonel.

WILKES (Frank Moorly). CONWAY 1915/16. Rank unknown.

MBE. Chances are he was Merchant Navy, aged 40 plus, Chief Officer or Master.

WOOLFENDEN (Joseph Eric). CONWAY 1924/26. Lieutenant, RNR.

MiD: 27/6/41. For outstanding zeal, patience and cheerfulness and never failing to set an example of wholehearted devotion to duty, without which the high tradition of the Royal Navy could not be upheld.

WORK (Magnus Spence). CONWAY 1926/27. Lieutenant-Commander, RNR.

DSC: 31/12/43. For gallantry and distinguished service in the face of the enemy. HMS DAHLIA was part of First Escort Group in the North Atlantic. He left DAHLIA, 28/12/43, and stood by BAMBOROUGH CASTLE.

BAR to DSC: 2/6/44. For outstanding leadership, skill and devotion to duty in HMS DAHLIA in successful actions with U-boats while on convoy escort duty in the Atlantic By this time Work was a Temporary Acting Lieutenant-Commander.

SECOND BAR to DSC: 16/3/45. For gallant service, endurance and devotion to duty while serving in HMS BAMBOROUGH CASTLE in Arctic seas while escorting convoys to and from Russia. He was the Commanding Officer from 28/3/44 to 11/3.45. U-387 was sunk in the Barents Sea on 9/12/44. Work was a highly successful Escort Captain, he never lost a man.

YOOL (William Munro). CONWAY 1908/10. Air Vice-Marshal, RAF.

CBE: 28/12/40. Group Captain Yool was stationed in the RAF Staff College. Joined RFC in 1915 and the RAF in 1919. He retired as Air Vice-Marshal, 1949.

CB: 28/12/45. Air Officer Commanding Administration in the Mediterranean and Middle East.

YOUNG (David). CONWAY 1940/42. Cadet, Merchant Navy.

MiD: 5/2/43. For gallantry, skill and resolution while an important convoy was fought through to Malta in the face of relentless attacks by day and night from enemy aircraft, submarines and surface forces.

WE WILL REMEMBER THEM

Names of former cadets who lost their lives in both World Wars were meticulously recorded on Memorial Boards. When the establishment closed the boards were saved and are now in the custody of The Friends of HMS CONWAY, located in Birkenhead.

The lists can only be tentative but were a genuine attempt to find the Old Conways who had made the ultimate sacrifice. A total of 160 names appear on World War One board. Assuming an annual intake of some one hundred Cadets and an upper age limit of, say, fifty-five for those liable to be in areas of danger during the war, this implies the casualty rate was 4.21%.

Quite a few young men were tempted to become aircrew in the RNAS, RFC and, latterly, the RAF ... a route which was to become popular with adventure-seeking CONWAY boys between the wars.

A total of 167 names for World War Two have been identified, most of which appear inscribed on the salvaged Honours Board.

Various web-sites were accessed to obtain details about ships, Air Force squadrons, and other service units in order to judge the circumstances attending a loss. There were some remarkable results: for instance that there were twenty-one Royal Air Force aircrew who were Old Conways, including

Group Captain B V Robinson (28/29), the holder of the DSO, DFC and Bar, and AFC, and Squadron Leader PWO (Boy) Mould, DFC and Bar … the first pilot to shoot down an enemy aircraft in 1939. A different, but tragic, tale is that of 40 years old Lieutenant Commander W E Fletcher Royal Navy (17/19) who lost his life to hypothermia when plunging into icy water in a vain attempt to rescue the famous woman aviator Amy Johnson when her plane crash-landed into the Thames … an action which led to the award of a posthumous ALBERT MEDAL. There were, of course, numerous casualties of the war at sea, including two highly decorated Atlantic Escort Group commanders: Lieutenant-Commanders J I Miller, DSO, DSC, RD (17/19) and H M C Sanders DSO, DSC, RD (16/18). Three Old Conways were lost when the great battle cruiser HMS HOOD blew up while being engaged by the German battle ship BISMARK in the Denmark Strait in May 1941: the youngest of these was 16 year old Probationary Temporary Midshipman M H P Freeman, RNR, who had only left CONWAY a few weeks previously that Easter.

Thirty-five Old Conways lost their lives in the Merchant Navy and their names are inscribed on the Memorial on Tower Hill, London, while there are another thirty-eight names who are unrecorded on any of the listings who may reasonably be presumed to have been in the Merchant Navy when they died, making a total of seventy-three Merchant Navy casualties in all.

WE WILL REMEMBER THEM